The Roman Emp

Augustus Caesar's Guide to Political Power

A.A. Castor

Table of Contents

The Roman Emperor's Playbook: Augustus Caesar's Guide to Political Power

A.A. Castor

Dedication

To my beloved family,
Your unconditional love, unwavering support, and endless encouragement have been my greatest blessings. From the earliest days of dreaming to the challenging moments of writing, you have stood by me with patience and belief. This book is as much yours as it is mine, a reflection of the values you've instilled and the faith you've shown in me. Thank you for being my rock and my inspiration.

To my dear friends,
Your friendship has illuminated my path with laughter, shared moments, and invaluable support. You've cheered me on through every triumph and lifted me up through every challenge. Your belief in my endeavors has been a source of strength and motivation. This book is a testament to the power of friendship, and I am grateful for each of you who has walked this journey by my side.

To God,
Your grace and guidance have been my constant companions. In moments of doubt, you've shown me the way; in moments of joy, you've multiplied my gratitude. This book is a testament to your faithfulness and the blessings you've bestowed upon me. May it serve as a reflection of your love and the lessons you continue to teach me.

With heartfelt gratitude and love,
A.A. Castor

Copyright © 2024 by A.A. Castor

Why I Am Writing This Book

The wisdom of people from the past, particularly leaders like Augustus, offers us invaluable lessons that transcend time. By examining the lives and strategies of historical figures, we gain insight into timeless principles of leadership, power, and governance that are as relevant today as they were thousands of years ago. Augustus, in particular, provides a fascinating study in how to navigate complex political landscapes, manage competing interests, and build systems that endure long after an individual's time. His ability to unite a fractured Roman Republic and transform it into a stable and prosperous empire is not just a historical feat, but a blueprint for leadership in any era.

In today's fast-paced, interconnected world, the lessons from Augustus' reign resonate more than ever. We live in a time where leaders face constant challenges—whether in politics, business, or social organizations. The complexity of managing relationships, perception, and influence is timeless, and Augustus mastered these elements in ways that continue to offer valuable guidance. He was able to adapt to changing circumstances, secure loyalty, and foster a legacy that ensured the continuity of his vision long after his death.

I am writing this book because I believe the wisdom of past leaders like Augustus provides us with a framework for understanding not only historical events but also the core principles of leadership that apply to today's world. The strategies he used to consolidate power, manage public perception, and create lasting institutions are still relevant in a world that demands both adaptability and stability. By reflecting on

Augustus' political genius, we can learn how to approach our own leadership challenges with a blend of foresight, pragmatism, and vision.

This book is meant to be more than just a historical account—it is a study of leadership that draws connections between ancient wisdom and modern challenges. The lessons Augustus left behind remind us that while the world has changed, the dynamics of power, influence, and leadership remain fundamentally the same. Whether one is leading a nation, a corporation, or a small team, the wisdom of the past offers us a lens through which we can better understand the present and prepare for the future.

.

Warning and Disclaimer

The information provided in this book is intended for educational and informational purposes only. While every effort has been made to ensure the accuracy and reliability of the content, the author and publisher make no representations or warranties regarding the completeness, accuracy, or applicability of the information presented. The strategies, insights, and historical examples discussed are based on personal interpretations and research and may not be universally applicable in all situations.

The author and publisher disclaim any liability for any loss, damage, or inconvenience arising from the use of the information in this book. Readers are encouraged to exercise their own judgment and seek professional advice when applying the lessons, strategies, or concepts discussed herein to their own personal or professional circumstances.

Neither the author nor the publisher shall be held liable for any direct or indirect consequences resulting from the use or misuse of the material presented in this book.

About the Author

A.A. Castor is a dedicated writer and researcher with a deep passion for exploring the intersection of history, leadership, and strategy. With a focus on uncovering timeless lessons from the past and applying them to contemporary challenges, Castor's work spans a range of topics from political strategy and philosophy to social dynamics and governance. His writing aims to bridge the gap between ancient wisdom and modern-day leadership, offering readers practical insights they can apply in both their personal and professional lives.

Drawing inspiration from historical figures such as Augustus Caesar, Castor delves into the strategies that have shaped civilizations and leaders for centuries. With a background in both historical study and leadership theory, his books are designed to engage readers with compelling narratives while providing actionable lessons that resonate in today's world.

When not writing, A.A. Castor enjoys podcasting on a variety of topics related to leadership, history, and social philosophy. His dedication to ongoing research ensures that his readers are always provided with well-rounded, thoughtful perspectives on the subjects he explores.

Introduction: The Legacy of Augustus Caesar

The end of the Roman Republic was a time of immense turmoil. Civil wars, political assassinations, and deep divisions threatened to dismantle the very fabric of Rome. In the midst of this chaos rose Augustus Caesar, a man who would not only restore order but fundamentally reshape the Roman world. Though initially seen as a young and untested heir to Julius Caesar, Augustus would become the architect of a new era—one defined by stability, prosperity, and the concentration of power in a single ruler.

Augustus' reign marked the beginning of the Roman Empire and the end of the Republic. But what set him apart was not just his political acumen, but his mastery in navigating the complex and often dangerous world of Roman politics. He understood the power of perception, presenting himself as the humble servant of the Republic while quietly consolidating control behind the scenes. He was a strategist, a reformer, and a manipulator when necessary—traits that allowed him to maintain a delicate balance between public approval and autocratic rule.

Augustus' legacy stretches beyond his lifetime. He crafted an image of leadership that would influence the empire for centuries and left behind structures that stabilized Rome long after his death. His careful combination of diplomacy, legal reforms, and military strength created a system that allowed him to rule effectively for over 40 years. More than a ruler, Augustus was a visionary who understood that true power lies not only in conquest but in the ability to manage and maintain control over the complexities of a vast and diverse empire.

As the founder of the Roman Empire, Augustus set the stage for what would become one of the most enduring political entities in history. His methods, though steeped in the politics of ancient Rome, offer enduring lessons for leadership, governance, and power that remain relevant even in modern times. Through his legacy, the world witnessed how one man, with a combination of genius and ruthlessness, could shape the course of history.

This book will explore the strategies Augustus used to rise from obscurity to supreme power, laying the groundwork for understanding the lasting impact of his rule.

Opening with Augustus' Legacy

SETTING THE STAGE: The End of the Roman Republic

Begin by introducing the historical landscape of Rome following Julius Caesar's assassination. The Republic, once a powerful political system, was in disarray. Civil wars, political infighting, and economic instability threatened to tear the state apart. Amid this chaos, Augustus emerged as the figure who would bring stability and create a lasting legacy.

The Rise of Augustus

Augustus, initially known as Octavian, was a relatively unknown figure before being named Julius Caesar's heir. Despite his youth and lack of experience, Augustus quickly demonstrated his ability to navigate Rome's dangerous political waters. With a keen sense for timing and alliances, he positioned himself as the leader who would restore order to the fractured Republic.

The Genius of Augustus: A Master of Strategy

Augustus' brilliance was not in military conquest alone, but in his ability to reshape the Roman political system from within. He was a master of subtlety, using political reforms, calculated alliances, and strategic displays of power to consolidate his authority while maintaining the illusion of republican governance.

- **Genius in Reform:** Augustus reformed the Roman government, restructuring the Senate and public offices to maintain the appearance of democracy while concentrating power in his own hands.

- **Genius in Image Crafting:** Augustus understood the importance of perception. He presented himself as the "first citizen," a servant of Rome, while using art, literature, and public works to solidify his image as the stabilizing force behind the empire's prosperity.

The Ruthlessness of Augustus: Cold and Calculated

While Augustus projected an image of benevolence and reform, he was also ruthless when necessary. Political opponents were systematically eliminated, either through assassination, exile, or legal manipulation. Augustus knew when to show clemency to win public favor and when to act decisively to remove threats to his rule.

- **Ruthless in War:** During the civil wars, Augustus fought strategic campaigns, including his decisive victory over Mark Antony and Cleopatra at Actium. His military actions were carefully calculated, ensuring his dominance without unnecessary risk.

- **Ruthless in Politics:** Politically, Augustus used every tool at his disposal, including the legal system, to neutralize rivals and consolidate his power. Former allies who outlived their usefulness were quietly sidelined or removed.

Lasting Impact: Shaping the Roman World

Augustus' reign not only stabilized Rome but laid the groundwork for the Pax Romana, a period of unprecedented peace and prosperity. His political and administrative reforms endured long after his death, influencing the Roman Empire for centuries. Augustus transformed Rome from a fractured Republic into a centralized, efficient empire that expanded its influence across the known world.

- **Pax Romana:** Under Augustus' leadership, the Roman Empire entered a golden age of peace and expansion. His policies created the conditions for economic growth, military success, and cultural flourishing.

- **The Augustus Myth:** Upon his death, Augustus was deified, cementing his legacy as more than just a political leader—he became a symbol of Rome's greatness. His name, "Augustus," became synonymous with power, dignity, and success, adopted by future emperors as a title of authority.

Concluding the Introduction:

Close by positioning Augustus as a timeless example of strategic leadership. His legacy endures not just in the monuments of ancient Rome, but in the political systems and leadership models that followed. Augustus was a figure who combined genius, foresight, and ruthlessness to reshape an entire world, and his strategies offer valuable lessons in leadership, power, and governance.

Comparison to Modern Politicians: Practical Power in Action

MASTER OF PUBLIC PERCEPTION

Augustus excelled in crafting a public image that balanced authority with humility. He was not just the ruler of an empire; he branded himself as the "restorer of the Republic" and a protector of Roman traditions. Modern politicians, similarly, often position themselves as defenders of the values their constituencies hold dear, while exercising considerable power behind the scenes. Augustus' use of media—statues, coins, and literary works like the *Aeneid*—can be likened to today's political campaigns, which use mass media and social platforms to shape a leader's public persona.

- **Modern Parallel:** Politicians today understand the importance of media influence and public relations. Like Augustus, they carefully manage their image, from press conferences to social media posts, to present themselves as relatable, trustworthy figures, while orchestrating major decisions in the background.

Strategic Alliances and Calculated Betrayals

Augustus built alliances when it served his goals, such as the formation of the Second Triumvirate with Mark Antony and Lepidus. However, when these alliances threatened his power, he dismantled them, often ruthlessly. Modern politicians follow a similar path—forming coalitions, political partnerships, or cross-party agreements to achieve short-term goals, but shifting allegiances or severing ties when those relationships are no longer beneficial.

- **Modern Parallel:** In modern politics, strategic alliances are a cornerstone of power-building. Politicians form alliances with interest groups, political parties, and international partners to gain support. However, they often break or modify these alliances when the political landscape changes, just as Augustus did.

Legal Manipulation to Secure Power

Augustus was a master of using the legal system to solidify his rule. His reforms to the Senate gave the appearance of restoring democratic governance while, in reality, concentrating power in his hands. Many modern politicians similarly use legislative systems to pass laws or enact reforms that strengthen their position while maintaining the appearance of democratic governance.

- **Modern Parallel:** Politicians today manipulate legal and bureaucratic structures to consolidate power—whether through executive orders, political appointments, or legislative changes. Like Augustus, they often work within the system, bending it to their advantage without overtly appearing authoritarian.

Ruthlessness Balanced with Compassion

Augustus eliminated rivals and quelled rebellions when necessary, but he also knew when to show clemency to preserve his image and win public favor. This balancing act between ruthlessness and compassion is seen in modern politics, where leaders must sometimes take hardline actions but balance them with policies that appeal to the masses.

- **Modern Parallel:** Leaders today may implement harsh policies (such as military action or tough economic sanctions) while simultaneously promoting social welfare programs or giving public speeches that emphasize empathy and compassion. This duality in leadership is key to maintaining authority and popularity, just as it was for Augustus.

Long-Term Legacy Building

Augustus wasn't focused solely on his time in power; he carefully planned for the future. He reformed Rome's institutions to endure long after his death, ensuring his legacy as the founder of the empire. Modern politicians similarly look to build legacies, whether through landmark policies, social programs, or reforms intended to shape future generations.

- **Modern Parallel:** Legacy building is a common theme among world leaders today. By passing significant legislation or initiating long-term projects, politicians aim to ensure that their influence and policies will last far beyond their terms in office, much like Augustus' establishment of the Pax Romana.

Conclusion: Effective, Not Theoretical

Augustus' strategies were not abstract theories but practical actions that reshaped the Roman Empire and secured his reign for decades. Modern politicians, whether consciously or unconsciously, follow many of the same tactics—manipulating alliances, controlling public perception, and using legal systems to their advantage. Augustus offers a template for how effective political leadership can be executed through a blend of cunning, pragmatism, and a long-term vision.

Why Augustus Still Matters

AUGUSTUS' METHODS FOR acquiring and maintaining power continue to be relevant today because they are based on timeless principles of leadership, strategy, and human nature. His ability to control the narrative, consolidate power behind the scenes, and manage both allies and enemies with precision demonstrates that political success is often about perception, manipulation, and long-term planning. Augustus understood that power isn't just about domination; it's about creating a system that supports your rule and ensures stability even after you're gone.

Augustus' understanding of public image and the importance of propaganda mirrors how modern leaders rely on media, messaging, and branding to connect with the masses. His skill in legal manipulation, using the Senate and Roman laws to cement his authority, shows how political systems can be used as tools to achieve one's goals while maintaining the illusion of fairness and democracy. This is reflected in today's politics, where leaders often work within existing legal frameworks to expand their power without appearing authoritarian.

His approach to alliances also remains significant. Augustus built partnerships when they were useful, and dissolved them when they no longer served his purposes. This ability to form and break alliances without losing control is critical for leaders in any era, especially when navigating complex political landscapes.

Finally, Augustus' legacy-building demonstrates the importance of planning for the future, ensuring that the structures he put in place lasted well beyond his lifetime. Modern leaders similarly strive to leave behind legacies that shape their nations or organizations for decades to come, understanding that true leadership is not just about short-term gains but about creating lasting impact.

In today's world, where politics, leadership, and public perception are more interconnected than ever, Augustus provides a blueprint for understanding how power can be gained, wielded, and preserved. His ability to balance ruthlessness with compassion, strategy with vision, and authority with public approval makes his leadership style a model for those seeking to understand the mechanics of power in any era.

This book will now explore the various strategies Augustus used to rise to the top and maintain control over one of the greatest empires in history. Through his example, we'll uncover practical lessons for navigating the complexities of modern leadership and governance.

Chapter 1: From Chaos to Control — Seizing Power in a Fragile Republic

The fall of the Roman Republic was not a sudden event, but a gradual unraveling of political structures that had once governed the most powerful state in the ancient world. Years of internal conflict, social upheaval, and civil war had left the Republic on the verge of collapse. The assassination of Julius Caesar in 44 BCE was the tipping point, plunging Rome into even deeper chaos. In this fragile environment, many sought to seize control, but few had the skill, patience, or vision to succeed.

It was in this volatile landscape that Augustus, then known as Octavian, emerged. At the age of 18, he was thrust into the center of Roman politics, seemingly unprepared for the immense challenge ahead. Yet, in the midst of the political chaos, Octavian saw an opportunity. Through a series of calculated moves, alliances, and decisive military actions, he would rise from an untested youth to become the sole ruler of Rome.

Octavian's journey from the margins of power to its pinnacle was not a straightforward path. It required him to navigate treacherous alliances, survive civil wars, and outmaneuver seasoned rivals. What set him apart was his ability to understand the fragility of the Republic and use its weaknesses to his advantage. Where others faltered or became consumed by ambition, Octavian remained focused on his ultimate goal: the consolidation of power under his control.

In a world where political survival depended on swift and often ruthless action, Octavian displayed a remarkable balance of patience and aggression. He used the Republic's instability to his benefit, presenting himself as the figure who could restore order and end the chaos that had gripped Rome for years. By the time he emerged as Augustus, the first Roman emperor, the Republic was no more, and in its place stood a new form of governance, one crafted to serve his ambition and ensure his legacy.

This chapter explores how Augustus seized power in a time of unprecedented fragility, turning chaos into control, and establishing a new order that would shape the Roman world for centuries to come.

Historical Context

THE ASSASSINATION OF Julius Caesar in 44 BCE plunged Rome into chaos. What had once been the most powerful Republic in the world was now a fractured state, torn apart by political infighting and civil war. Senators who had orchestrated Caesar's death believed they were saving the Republic from dictatorship, but instead, they unleashed a period of instability and violence. With no clear leader and various factions vying for control, Rome became a battleground for power.

In the wake of this turmoil, an unlikely figure began to rise—Gaius Octavius, the grand-nephew of Julius Caesar. At the time of Caesar's death, Octavian was just 18 years old, inexperienced, and far from the political epicenter of Rome. Yet, he had been named Caesar's heir in his will, a revelation that immediately thrust him into the public eye. Octavian quickly took the name Gaius Julius Caesar Octavianus, aligning himself with the legacy of his great-uncle. Despite his youth and lack of military experience, he understood that his claim to power rested on his ability to navigate Rome's dangerous political landscape.

Octavian's rise was anything but simple. He had to contend with the likes of Mark Antony, one of Caesar's closest allies and a seasoned general, who initially dismissed Octavian as a political lightweight. But Octavian was far more calculating than his opponents realized. Through a combination of strategic alliances, political maneuvering, and a shrewd understanding of Roman public sentiment, he began to gain influence. He used the promise of avenging Julius Caesar's death as a rallying cry, aligning himself with the public's desire for stability and retribution against the conspirators.

Octavian's early moves were masterful. He formed the Second Triumvirate with Mark Antony and Lepidus, a temporary alliance designed to consolidate power and eliminate mutual enemies. Together, they defeated the forces of Brutus and Cassius, the chief conspirators in Caesar's assassination, at the Battle of Philippi in 42 BCE. This victory gave Octavian military credibility and strengthened his position in Roman politics.

However, Octavian's true genius lay in his ability to outmaneuver his allies. He gradually marginalized Lepidus, removing him from power, and set the stage for a final confrontation with Mark Antony. As Antony's relationship with Cleopatra deepened, Octavian skillfully used Roman fears of foreign influence to turn the Senate and public opinion against him. The ensuing Battle of Actium in 31 BCE marked the end of Antony and Cleopatra's forces, and with their defeat, Octavian became the undisputed ruler of Rome.

In less than two decades, Octavian had transformed himself from a relatively unknown heir into Augustus Caesar, Rome's first emperor. His rise to power was a testament to his political cunning, his understanding of the Roman people, and his ability to seize opportunities in the midst of chaos.

Shrewd Political Moves

ONE OF AUGUSTUS' MOST decisive and shrewd moves was his immediate alignment with the legacy of Julius Caesar. Upon learning that his great-uncle had been assassinated and that he had been named Caesar's heir in his will, the young Octavian recognized the significance of this opportunity. By adopting the name Gaius Julius Caesar Octavianus, he made a bold and calculated decision to associate himself with one of the most powerful and influential figures in Roman history. In doing so, he positioned himself as the legitimate successor, not just in familial terms, but in the eyes of the Roman people and Caesar's loyal legions.

The political landscape at the time was fraught with uncertainty. Julius Caesar's assassination had left a vacuum of power, and many feared the return of the chaotic civil wars that had plagued Rome for decades. Octavian was relatively unknown and unproven, but by claiming the title "Caesar's heir," he tapped into the immense loyalty and reverence that many Romans still held for Caesar. This move instantly gave him political and symbolic authority, despite his youth and inexperience.

More than just a name change, Octavian's adoption of Caesar's title was a calculated strategy to secure early legitimacy. It allowed him to rally support from Caesar's veterans and military commanders, particularly those stationed in key provinces like Gaul and Hispania, who were still loyal to their fallen leader. Octavian's ability to invoke Caesar's memory became a powerful tool, as he presented himself as the avenger of Caesar's murder, calling for justice against the conspirators who had plunged Rome into chaos.

Octavian further cemented his claim by utilizing Caesar's wealth to fund his growing political campaign. Caesar's vast estate, now his by inheritance, gave him the financial means to build a power base, pay soldiers, and buy political favor in Rome. This financial backing was crucial in gaining support from both the Senate and the military, as it allowed Octavian to present himself not just as an heir in name, but as a practical leader with the resources to carry out his plans.

This decision to adopt Caesar's legacy also helped Octavian stand in contrast to his chief rival, Mark Antony, who was seen as a more seasoned politician but one who was increasingly distant from Rome due to his involvement with Cleopatra in Egypt. By aligning himself closely with Caesar's memory, Octavian was able to present himself as the true protector of Rome's interests and the legitimate continuator of Caesar's vision, while subtly painting Antony as a man distracted by foreign entanglements.

In essence, Octavian's decision to become "Caesar's heir" was far more than a symbolic gesture—it was a strategic masterstroke that allowed him to leverage the deep well of public and military support for Julius Caesar. It gave him the foundation upon which he would build his political career and, eventually, his transformation into Augustus, the first emperor of Rome. This early move demonstrated his ability to seize opportunities, control public perception, and establish himself as a key player in Roman politics at a time when the future of the Republic hung in the balance.

Navigating Civil Wars

AUGUSTUS' RISE TO POWER was marked by his strategic involvement in a series of civil wars that ultimately allowed him to eliminate rivals and solidify his influence over Rome. Each conflict was carefully navigated to serve his long-term goals, using military force, propaganda, and political maneuvering to emerge victorious while presenting himself as a stabilizing figure for the Republic.

After forming the Second Triumvirate with Mark Antony and Lepidus in 43 BCE, Augustus (then Octavian) entered into a power-sharing arrangement that would eventually dissolve as he outmaneuvered his allies. The Triumvirate was initially successful in its goal of defeating the assassins of Julius Caesar, most notably Brutus and Cassius, at the Battle of Philippi in 42 BCE. This victory was a key moment for Augustus, as it allowed him to claim vengeance for Caesar's death and present himself as a true protector of Caesar's legacy. It also gave him military credibility, which was essential for a leader in a culture where military success equaled political power.

However, Augustus knew that the alliance with Antony and Lepidus was temporary and filled with tension. He recognized that the real contest for control of Rome would come from within, particularly between himself and Mark Antony, who had long been one of Caesar's most trusted generals and held significant influence in the eastern provinces. Instead of confronting Antony immediately, Augustus bided his time, consolidating his power in the west, where he built up his military resources and political alliances. At the same time, he worked to marginalize Lepidus, stripping him of his territories after an ill-advised revolt in 36 BCE, effectively removing him as a contender.

The final showdown came in the form of a civil war between Augustus and Mark Antony, whose alliance with Cleopatra, Queen of Egypt, became the centerpiece of Augustus' propaganda campaign. By emphasizing Antony's foreign entanglements and romantic involvement with Cleopatra, Augustus portrayed Antony as a man who had abandoned Roman values and was under the influence of a foreign queen. This narrative struck a chord with Roman society, which feared the growing influence of Egypt and saw Antony's actions as a betrayal of Rome.

Augustus' use of propaganda in this conflict was masterful. He framed the war not as a personal power struggle but as a defense of Rome against foreign domination, with Antony depicted as a traitor. By shifting the focus from a civil war to a war against a foreign adversary (Cleopatra and Egypt), Augustus was able to secure broad support from both the Senate and the Roman people. This manipulation of public sentiment proved to be a turning point in the conflict.

The decisive moment came at the Battle of Actium in 31 BCE. Augustus' forces, led by his trusted general Agrippa, defeated Antony and Cleopatra's fleet, securing his control over the Mediterranean. Antony and Cleopatra fled to Egypt, where they eventually committed suicide, leaving Augustus as the uncontested ruler of Rome. The victory at Actium was more than just a military triumph—it marked the end of the Roman Republic's chaotic civil wars and the beginning of Augustus' undisputed reign.

Each of these civil wars acted as stepping stones for Augustus. Rather than rushing into conflicts, he carefully chose his battles, built alliances, and used public perception to his advantage. By eliminating rivals like Brutus, Cassius, Lepidus, and finally Antony, Augustus systematically removed every obstacle to his path to power. His ability to navigate these civil wars demonstrated his patience, strategic thinking, and willingness to use both force and diplomacy when necessary. Ultimately, it allowed him to transition from a leader in a fractured political system to the first emperor of Rome, ending the Republic and founding a new era of imperial rule under his control.

Key Takeaway: Seizing Opportunities in Chaos

AUGUSTUS' RISE TO POWER provides a masterclass in how moments of instability and chaos can be turned into opportunities for control and consolidation of power. His ascent was not marked by brute force alone, but by carefully calculated decisions, timing, and adaptability in the face of ever-changing political landscapes. There are several crucial lessons that emerge from his ability to navigate these tumultuous periods:

1. **Recognizing Opportunity in Chaos**: Augustus knew that the disorder following Julius Caesar's assassination presented a unique opportunity. Instead of being overwhelmed by the instability, he positioned himself as the solution to the chaos. Similarly, in any period of upheaval, whether in politics, business, or personal leadership, recognizing when disorder can be used to your advantage is crucial. Augustus saw the potential in becoming Caesar's heir, a move that provided immediate legitimacy in a time when Rome was looking for stability.

2. **Strategic Patience**: Augustus understood that timing is everything. He didn't rush into conflicts but waited for the right moment to strike. In the early years of the Second Triumvirate, he allowed Antony and Lepidus to make their moves while he consolidated his power in the west. He didn't engage Antony directly until he had built up the necessary military strength and public support. Leaders today can learn from this patience—sometimes the best move is to wait, gather resources, and let your rivals expose their weaknesses before acting.

3. **Adaptability**: One of Augustus' greatest strengths was his ability to adapt to the changing political and military

circumstances. As civil wars broke out and alliances shifted, Augustus remained flexible, adjusting his strategies as necessary. When Antony allied with Cleopatra, Augustus adapted his propaganda to paint Antony as a foreign threat. His ability to pivot quickly to match new realities was key to his success. In today's fast-changing world, adaptability is equally vital for leaders to navigate crises and maintain control.

4. **Control the Narrative**: Augustus understood that winning wars wasn't just about military victories—it was about controlling the public narrative. He used propaganda to paint himself as the defender of Roman values and Antony as a traitor under the influence of a foreign queen. Leaders who control the narrative in times of instability are often the ones who emerge on top. Crafting a message that resonates with the public, especially in times of uncertainty, can turn the tide in your favor.

5. **Consolidation of Power After Victory**: Augustus knew that gaining power through military victory was only the first step. After the Battle of Actium, he was careful to consolidate his power by maintaining the appearance of restoring the Republic, all while establishing a system where he held ultimate control. This consolidation ensured that his reign would be secure, and it laid the foundation for decades of peace and stability. Similarly, leaders must understand that winning in a moment of crisis is just the beginning—the true test of power is in how it is maintained and institutionalized afterward.

Lesson in Leadership: Augustus' rise illustrates that moments of chaos are fertile ground for those who can remain calm, strategic, and adaptive. Recognizing opportunities, carefully timing actions, and maintaining flexibility are essential skills for any leader looking to consolidate power and create lasting influence.

Chapter 2: The Art of Alliance — Building and Breaking Partnerships

Alliances are at the heart of any successful pursuit of power, whether in politics, business, or warfare. In the chaotic and volatile world of ancient Rome, Augustus understood this better than anyone. He knew that, in order to rise through the ranks of a fractured and tumultuous Republic, he would need to forge strategic partnerships. However, he also recognized that these alliances were not meant to last forever. They were tools—valuable in the short term, but ultimately expendable once they had served their purpose.

Augustus' ascent to absolute power was not accomplished through sheer force alone, but through his ability to skillfully manage relationships. He allied himself with some of the most powerful figures of his time, including Mark Antony and Lepidus, using their influence to eliminate mutual enemies and establish a foothold in Roman politics. But as his ambitions grew, so too did his need to break away from those very alliances that had helped him rise. Augustus knew when to form partnerships, but more importantly, he knew when to end them without igniting unnecessary conflict or undermining his own position.

This delicate balance of building and breaking alliances defined Augustus' approach to power. His ability to manipulate partnerships for his own benefit while remaining outwardly cooperative was a key factor in his transformation from a relatively unknown heir to Julius Caesar into the sole ruler of the Roman Empire. This chapter delves into Augustus' masterful handling of alliances, exploring how he formed critical partnerships, leveraged them to his advantage, and eventually dismantled them to secure his place as Rome's first emperor.

The Second Triumvirate

THE FORMATION OF THE Second Triumvirate in 43 BCE was a pivotal moment in Augustus' rise to power. In the immediate aftermath of Julius Caesar's assassination, Rome was in disarray, with no clear path forward for any one individual to seize control. Augustus, Mark Antony, and Lepidus—each with their own ambitions—came together in a strategic alliance that would temporarily stabilize the political situation and allow them to focus on their common enemies, the conspirators behind Caesar's murder.

The Second Triumvirate was not merely an informal agreement; it was a legally sanctioned power-sharing arrangement, ratified by the Roman Senate, which granted each of the three men extraordinary powers to rule Rome and its territories. This arrangement gave Augustus, Antony, and Lepidus control over vast resources, armies, and provinces, dividing the Roman world into spheres of influence that they would govern. Augustus, despite his youth and relative inexperience, was able to secure control of the western provinces, while Antony controlled the east and Lepidus the African territories.

For Augustus, this alliance served as a means to an end. He understood that, while the Second Triumvirate was a necessary step in consolidating power, it would not last forever. His initial goal was to work within the triumvirate to eliminate the immediate threats to their rule, particularly the forces of Brutus and Cassius, who had led the assassination of Julius Caesar and were rallying support to challenge the triumvirs. Augustus recognized the importance of securing military victories and, through the combined efforts of the triumvirate, the Battle of Philippi in 42 BCE saw the defeat of Brutus and Cassius, cementing the triumvirs' control over Rome.

However, Augustus was always mindful of the dynamics within the triumvirate itself. While publicly presenting a unified front with Antony and Lepidus, he began to subtly position himself for greater power. He was careful to strengthen his base in the western provinces, cultivating loyalty among his soldiers and securing the support of influential Roman families. Augustus also used his connection to Julius Caesar, continuously promoting himself as Caesar's rightful heir, a move that further endeared him to the Roman public and Caesar's former legions.

Antony, meanwhile, was focused on the eastern provinces and became increasingly tied to Cleopatra, the Queen of Egypt, a relationship that would later become a source of tension between him and Augustus. Lepidus, the least influential of the three, gradually found himself sidelined as Augustus and Antony vied for supremacy.

The Second Triumvirate was a temporary but crucial phase in Augustus' rise. It allowed him to eliminate key rivals, build alliances, and solidify his position as a legitimate power in Rome. Yet even as he cooperated with Antony and Lepidus, Augustus was laying the groundwork for his eventual dominance. He skillfully worked within the alliance, knowing that the real contest for control of Rome would come once their common enemies were defeated. This partnership, while instrumental in securing immediate military victories, was always viewed by Augustus as a stepping stone toward his ultimate goal: becoming the sole ruler of Rome.

By the time the Second Triumvirate began to fracture, Augustus had already positioned himself as the strongest member of the alliance, ready to take advantage of the inevitable power struggle that would follow.

Strategic Use of Marriage

AUGUSTUS' MARRIAGES were not just personal decisions but carefully crafted political maneuvers that played a significant role in his rise to power. Like many rulers of the time, Augustus understood that marriage was a powerful tool to form alliances, strengthen political ties, and secure legitimacy. His marriages to Scribonia and later Livia Drusilla were strategic moves that bolstered his position in Roman society, allowed him to cultivate crucial political connections, and helped solidify his status as Rome's future ruler.

Augustus' first marriage to Scribonia, in 40 BCE, was a purely political alliance. Scribonia was closely related to Sextus Pompey, a powerful Roman general who controlled Sicily and posed a significant threat to the triumvirs' authority. By marrying Scribonia, Augustus sought to secure a temporary peace with Pompey and neutralize his potential opposition. This union allowed Augustus to focus on other enemies and stabilize his control over key provinces. However, the marriage was short-lived, lasting only a year and ending in divorce soon after Scribonia gave birth to Augustus' only biological child, Julia.

The marriage to Scribonia served its purpose, but once Augustus no longer needed the alliance with Pompey, he moved swiftly to end it. His decision to divorce Scribonia and marry Livia Drusilla was not only a personal choice but a political masterstroke that significantly strengthened his long-term position. Livia came from one of Rome's most prestigious and influential families, the Claudii. She was already married to Tiberius Claudius Nero, but Augustus, recognizing the potential value of this connection, arranged for her divorce and married her in 38 BCE, despite the fact that she was pregnant with her previous husband's child at the time.

The marriage to Livia brought Augustus into the powerful Claudian family, one of the most distinguished patrician lines in Rome. This connection gave him access to an influential network of political allies and social capital, further cementing his legitimacy and enhancing his standing among Rome's elite. Livia herself was a formidable figure—intelligent, politically astute, and deeply involved in Augustus' reign. She became a trusted advisor and partner, helping to manage domestic affairs and solidify the imperial family's influence.

Livia's sons from her previous marriage, Tiberius and Drusus, were also valuable additions to Augustus' political circle. While Augustus initially had his daughter Julia from his previous marriage, Livia's sons provided Augustus with potential heirs who could continue his legacy. Over time, Augustus would carefully groom Livia's son Tiberius for leadership, ultimately adopting him as his successor, ensuring the continuation of the Julio-Claudian dynasty.

Through these marriages, Augustus skillfully navigated the complex world of Roman politics, leveraging family connections to gain political advantages and secure his authority. His first marriage to Scribonia was a temporary alliance that served its purpose before being discarded, while his second marriage to Livia provided him with a long-term political partner and strengthened his ties to one of Rome's most powerful families. These strategic marriages were essential to Augustus' consolidation of power, demonstrating his ability to use personal relationships for political gain and ensuring his dominance in Roman politics for decades to come.

Ending Alliances When Necessary

AS AUGUSTUS SOLIDIFIED his power, he knew that the Second Triumvirate, while useful in the beginning, could not last indefinitely. His partners, Mark Antony and Lepidus, were rivals as much as they were allies, and Augustus understood that to become the sole ruler of Rome, he would eventually need to eliminate them from the equation. With patience and precision, Augustus dismantled the Triumvirate by first neutralizing Lepidus and then strategically isolating Mark Antony, ensuring his path to absolute control.

Lepidus was the first to fall. Though initially a key figure in the triumvirate, his power and influence steadily declined as Augustus and Antony consolidated their own territories. By 36 BCE, Lepidus made a critical misstep by attempting to seize control of Sicily after the defeat of Sextus Pompey. This move provided Augustus with the perfect opportunity to eliminate Lepidus as a political rival. Lepidus' soldiers, many of whom were loyal to Augustus, defected, leaving Lepidus powerless. Augustus stripped him of his titles and exiled him to a comfortable but politically irrelevant retirement, effectively removing him from the playing field without creating a public outcry or violent confrontation. In one swift move, Augustus had reduced the triumvirate to just two men: himself and Mark Antony.

With Lepidus neutralized, Augustus shifted his focus to Mark Antony, who remained a formidable rival. While the two men had cooperated to defeat their common enemies, their partnership had always been strained. Antony's growing involvement with Cleopatra, the powerful Queen of Egypt, provided Augustus with the leverage he needed to undermine Antony's position in Rome. Antony's relationship with Cleopatra, both personal and political, gave Augustus an opportunity to paint Antony as a man who had abandoned Roman values and was being seduced by foreign influence.

Augustus masterfully used propaganda to turn Roman public opinion against Antony. He depicted Antony as a traitor to Rome, a man more concerned with Cleopatra and Egypt than with the needs of the Roman people. By framing Antony's alliance with Cleopatra as a betrayal, Augustus tapped into the deeply ingrained Roman fear of foreign domination, casting Antony as a man willing to place Egypt's interests above Rome's. Augustus also used Antony's will, which had been stolen by his allies, to further discredit him. In it, Antony supposedly declared his desire to be buried in Alexandria, alongside Cleopatra, rather than in Rome. This revelation shocked the Roman Senate and public, reinforcing the idea that Antony had forsaken Rome for the allure of Cleopatra and her eastern kingdom.

With the public and the Senate increasingly hostile toward Antony, Augustus declared war—not directly on Antony, but on Cleopatra, framing it as a war to protect Roman sovereignty against a foreign threat. This move was politically astute, as it allowed Augustus to position himself as the defender of Rome, while casting Antony as merely a misguided pawn of Cleopatra. By focusing the conflict on Cleopatra, Augustus avoided the appearance of another internal civil war and presented it instead as a campaign to protect Roman values.

The decisive confrontation came at the Battle of Actium in 31 BCE, where Augustus' forces, led by his trusted general Agrippa, decisively defeated the combined forces of Antony and Cleopatra. Antony and Cleopatra fled to Egypt, where they eventually took their own lives, leaving Augustus the uncontested ruler of Rome. By this point, Augustus had fully isolated Antony, both militarily and politically, using their past alliance as a stepping stone to secure his own dominance.

Augustus' ability to dismantle the Triumvirate was a testament to his strategic foresight and political savvy. He methodically neutralized his rivals when they were no longer useful, removing Lepidus without conflict and turning the Roman people and Senate against Antony through a well-executed propaganda campaign. By the time he emerged victorious, Augustus had effectively eliminated every major rival, paving the way for his reign as Rome's first emperor. His handling of the Triumvirate's dissolution demonstrated a crucial lesson in leadership: knowing when to end alliances and how to do so without inciting backlash or creating new enemies.

Key Takeaway: The Importance of Strategic Alliances and Knowing When to End Them

AUGUSTUS' PATH TO BECOMING Rome's first emperor underscores the critical role that alliances can play in achieving short-term objectives, but equally highlights the necessity of ending or manipulating them when the time is right for long-term dominance. His creation of the Second Triumvirate with Mark Antony and Lepidus was a calculated move that provided him with the military resources, legitimacy, and public support needed to consolidate power in a time of uncertainty. This alliance allowed him to eliminate the immediate threats posed by Julius Caesar's assassins, Brutus and Cassius, and stabilize his position in Roman politics, all while avoiding direct conflict with powerful rivals in the early stages of his rise.

However, Augustus always recognized that alliances are temporary tools, not permanent solutions. He understood that as long as he shared power with Antony and Lepidus, he could never truly control Rome. His strategy was not to remain in a position of parity, but to surpass his partners. The careful dismantling of the Triumvirate shows the importance of knowing when to shift from cooperation to competition and how to manage the fallout of ending an alliance.

The first key to Augustus' success was his handling of Lepidus. Rather than confronting him with open hostility, Augustus waited for the right moment—an ill-advised move by Lepidus to seize Sicily—which provided him with a justifiable reason to strip Lepidus of power. This maneuver allowed Augustus to neutralize a rival without engaging in a costly civil war or provoking backlash from the Senate or the people. By framing Lepidus' fall as the result of his own actions, Augustus eliminated him quietly and effectively, showcasing a critical lesson: it is often more advantageous to let an ally discredit themselves, rather than openly attacking them.

The second key was Augustus' strategic manipulation of Mark Antony's relationship with Cleopatra. Recognizing that a direct military confrontation with Antony would risk civil unrest and divide Roman loyalties, Augustus instead chose to undermine Antony's public image. He masterfully used propaganda to paint Antony as a man under the sway of a foreign queen, betraying Roman values in favor of Egyptian interests. This move allowed Augustus to turn the Senate and Roman people against Antony without appearing as the aggressor. By framing the conflict as a defense of Roman honor against foreign influence, Augustus ensured that when the final clash came at the Battle of Actium, he had the full backing of Rome behind him.

The wisdom in Augustus' approach lies in his understanding that alliances serve a purpose but must be ended or manipulated when they begin to stand in the way of ultimate power. Forming partnerships can provide the means to achieve short-term goals—such as consolidating power, gaining military support, or neutralizing mutual enemies—but these alliances must be evaluated continuously. Augustus demonstrated that successful leadership requires not only the ability to create alliances but the insight to recognize when they have outlived their usefulness.

Knowing when and how to break an alliance is just as important as forming it. Augustus didn't simply dissolve the Triumvirate through brute force; he used patience, public perception, and strategic timing. He waited for Lepidus to make a mistake and for Antony to become vulnerable due to his foreign ties, allowing Augustus to eliminate his rivals in a way that minimized opposition and secured his dominance. By controlling the narrative and carefully managing each step, Augustus was able to break his alliances without triggering widespread resentment or backlash.

For modern leaders, Augustus' actions offer critical lessons: alliances are powerful but temporary tools. They must be used strategically for short-term gains, but as circumstances change, a leader must be prepared to dissolve or manipulate those alliances to avoid being constrained by them. Moreover, the manner in which alliances are ended is just as important as the decision to end them. When handled with care, the dissolution of partnerships can pave the way for long-term success, while poorly managed breakups can create lasting animosity and unforeseen challenges.

In essence, Augustus' rise to power teaches that in both politics and leadership, knowing when to ally and when to sever those ties is essential. Alliances can build momentum and establish a foothold, but true dominance comes from the ability to evolve beyond those relationships when they are no longer advantageous. Augustus' strategic dismantling of the Triumvirate was a masterclass in using alliances for short-term gains and breaking them at precisely the right moment to ensure his lasting supremacy.

Chapter 3: The Power of Perception — Creating a Public Image

The rise of Augustus from a relatively unknown heir to Julius Caesar to the first emperor of Rome was not due to military might or political maneuvering alone. A key element of his success was his unparalleled ability to control how he was perceived by the Roman people, the Senate, and the broader empire. Augustus understood that power was not just something to be seized through force; it was something that had to be maintained through careful manipulation of public image.

In a society as politically volatile as Rome, where the slightest misstep could lead to assassination or revolt, Augustus mastered the art of perception. He didn't just rule; he shaped how people viewed his rule. Every public act, every speech, and every monument he built was designed to reinforce his image as a benevolent and rightful leader. Whether through coins bearing his image, grand public works that beautified Rome, or literary works like Virgil's *Aeneid* that tied his reign to the divine will of the gods, Augustus crafted a narrative of himself as the savior of Rome, the man who brought peace and stability after decades of civil war.

The power of perception allowed Augustus to do what no other Roman leader had accomplished: he consolidated near-absolute power without appearing as a tyrant. By presenting himself as a humble "first citizen" and a servant of the Roman people, Augustus was able to build an empire while maintaining the loyalty of both the Senate and the citizens. He understood that in order to rule effectively, he had to win not just the wars on the battlefield, but the war of public opinion.

This chapter explores how Augustus used media, art, and culture to create an enduring public image that solidified his reign and ensured the stability of Rome. Through the manipulation of perception, Augustus controlled the narrative surrounding his rule, creating a model of leadership that would be emulated for centuries to come.

The "Restorer of the Republic" Myth

ONE OF AUGUSTUS' MOST brilliant and enduring political strategies was the crafting of his image as the "Restorer of the Republic." While he effectively dismantled the Republican system to consolidate power, Augustus skillfully portrayed himself not as a dictator or tyrant, but as the guardian of Rome's traditional values and institutions. This public persona allowed him to gain widespread support from the Roman Senate and people, all while slowly and quietly centralizing authority in his own hands.

In the wake of decades of civil wars and political upheaval, Rome was weary of conflict and instability. The Republic, which had been the foundation of Roman governance for centuries, was on the verge of collapse. The assassination of Julius Caesar, who had declared himself "dictator for life," created widespread fear of any leader who appeared to be seeking absolute power. Augustus, recognizing the fragile state of Roman politics and the deep-seated fears of despotism, took a different approach.

Rather than openly seizing power, Augustus presented himself as the opposite of Caesar—someone who sought to restore the traditional Republican order. In 27 BCE, after defeating Mark Antony and consolidating his military dominance, Augustus dramatically "returned" his powers to the Senate, claiming that the Republic had been restored. This act was a calculated move to gain the approval of the Senate and to avoid the mistakes that had led to his predecessor's downfall. By appearing to relinquish control, Augustus gave the impression that he had no personal ambition for dictatorial power and was merely acting in Rome's best interests.

However, this public renunciation of power was largely symbolic. In reality, Augustus retained control over the key instruments of power. He accepted titles such as "Princeps" (first citizen) and "Imperator" (commander), which gave him direct control over the military, the provinces, and the legislative process. Augustus also took on the position of *Pontifex Maximus* (chief priest), thereby wielding significant religious influence. By accepting these roles, he maintained effective autocratic control, but cloaked it in the language of Republican tradition.

The genius of this strategy lay in its subtlety. Augustus carefully avoided titles like "king" or "dictator," which would have alarmed the Senate and the Roman people. Instead, he framed his rule as the preservation of Roman customs and institutions, ensuring that his consolidation of power was gradual and largely unchallenged. This portrayal of himself as a servant of the Republic, rather than its ruler, allowed him to avoid the fate of Julius Caesar, whose blatant accumulation of power had led to his assassination.

Over time, the Republic that Augustus claimed to have restored became little more than a façade. The Senate still existed, but it had become largely ceremonial, with its decisions and actions subject to Augustus' approval. While the appearance of Republican governance remained, Augustus had effectively transformed the state into a monarchy in all but name. His power was absolute, but the myth that he was merely the "first citizen" ensured that his rule was accepted by the elite and the masses alike.

By crafting the "Restorer of the Republic" myth, Augustus managed to balance the need for control with the Roman people's aversion to despotism. He slowly eroded the true mechanisms of Republican governance while maintaining the illusion that they were still intact. This careful manipulation of public perception not only allowed Augustus to secure his own power but also created a model of leadership that would endure for centuries in the Roman Empire.

Augustus' ability to present himself as the defender of the Republic while consolidating autocratic power stands as one of the most successful political strategies in history. It demonstrates the importance of perception in leadership—how a ruler can maintain control not just through force, but through carefully managing their image and the expectations of their people.

The Role of Media in Rome

AUGUSTUS WAS ACUTELY aware of the power of media and public image, even in ancient times. Long before the age of mass communication, he effectively used the tools available—art, coins, monuments, and literature—to shape how the Roman people and the broader empire perceived him. Augustus understood that his authority was not only derived from his political and military control but also from the narrative that surrounded his reign. By controlling this narrative, he could reinforce his image as Rome's protector, the "restorer of the Republic," and a divinely favored ruler.

One of Augustus' most visible uses of media was through the widespread production of coins bearing his image. These coins, which circulated across the empire, served as everyday reminders of his authority. But Augustus didn't simply stamp his likeness on currency; he carefully crafted the messages these coins conveyed. Some coins depicted him as a youthful and vigorous leader, while others portrayed symbols of peace, victory, and prosperity, such as laurel wreaths and images of the goddess Pax. By linking his image with these symbols, Augustus reinforced the idea that his reign had brought stability and prosperity to Rome after years of civil war. Coins were more than currency—they were propaganda in the hands of every Roman citizen.

Augustus also used monumental architecture and public art to communicate his power and divine favor. Throughout Rome, he commissioned grand public works, including temples, forums, and other structures that not only improved the city but also glorified his rule. The most famous of these is the Ara Pacis, or Altar of Peace, which was built to celebrate the peace that Augustus had supposedly restored to the empire. Its intricate reliefs depict scenes of Roman prosperity and Augustus' family, symbolizing the continuity and future security of his rule. Public monuments like these helped Augustus embed his image in the fabric of Roman daily life, creating a physical legacy of his reign.

In addition to coins and monuments, Augustus used literature to shape his legacy, and no work was more important in this regard than Virgil's *Aeneid*. Commissioned by Augustus or heavily encouraged by his regime, *The Aeneid* was a masterful piece of political propaganda wrapped in an epic poem. It tells the story of Aeneas, a Trojan hero who escapes the destruction of Troy and eventually becomes the founder of the Roman people. By linking the mythical origins of Rome to the divine, Virgil crafted a narrative that emphasized Rome's greatness as preordained by the gods, with Augustus positioned as the natural continuation of this divine legacy.

The *Aeneid* was particularly powerful because it tied Augustus to the virtues of Aeneas—piety, duty, and leadership—thus framing his rule as the fulfillment of Rome's destiny. In one pivotal moment, Aeneas visits the underworld, where he meets the spirit of his descendants, including Augustus himself. In this scene, Augustus is presented as a divinely chosen ruler who will lead Rome to an era of unprecedented peace and prosperity, solidifying his legitimacy as the rightful leader of the empire.

Moreover, Virgil's *Aeneid* gave Augustus the historical and divine legitimacy he sought by tracing his lineage back to the gods. It reinforced Augustus' claim that he was not only restoring Rome but guiding it toward its ultimate and preordained greatness. By associating himself with Aeneas—a hero beloved by the gods and fated to found Rome—Augustus effectively positioned his rule as part of a grand, divine plan.

Augustus also encouraged other poets and writers, such as Horace and Ovid, to celebrate his reign and Rome's achievements under his leadership. Their works often praised the peace, stability, and prosperity that Augustus had brought to Rome, creating a cultural environment that continuously reinforced his image as a benevolent and divinely supported ruler.

In short, Augustus skillfully used the media of his time to shape how he was perceived throughout the Roman Empire. Whether through coins, art, architecture, or literature, he controlled the narrative surrounding his rule, ensuring that his image as the restorer of peace and a divinely chosen leader was constantly promoted. The *Aeneid* in particular played a crucial role in embedding Augustus' legacy within Rome's cultural and historical identity, presenting him as the rightful and destined ruler of a newly prosperous empire.

Through these media, Augustus transformed himself from a political figure into an almost mythic symbol of Rome's greatness, a reputation that would endure long after his death. His mastery of public image and propaganda ensured that his reign was not just remembered for its political achievements, but also for the powerful narrative of peace, restoration, and divine favor that he so carefully cultivated.

Public Works and Infrastructure

ONE OF AUGUSTUS' MOST enduring legacies was his ambitious program of public works and infrastructure, which transformed Rome from a city in decline into a gleaming capital of an empire. These projects not only improved the lives of Roman citizens but also served as a powerful tool for Augustus to bolster his image as a benevolent ruler and restorer of Rome's greatness. Through the construction of temples, roads, aqueducts, and public buildings, Augustus solidified his standing among the people while creating a lasting physical legacy that symbolized the stability and prosperity of his reign.

Augustus inherited a Rome that had been ravaged by decades of civil war. The city's infrastructure was crumbling, and the urban landscape was a chaotic mix of dilapidated buildings and poorly maintained streets. Recognizing the symbolic importance of restoring Rome to its former glory, Augustus embarked on a massive public works program designed to beautify the city, improve its functionality, and, importantly, leave a lasting imprint of his leadership. He famously claimed, "I found Rome a city of bricks and left it a city of marble," a statement that underscored the transformative impact of his building projects.

One of Augustus' primary focuses was the construction and restoration of temples and religious monuments. By rebuilding or refurbishing key temples, such as the Temple of Mars Ultor (Mars the Avenger) and the Temple of Apollo on the Palatine Hill, Augustus associated himself with Rome's traditional religious values and the gods. These structures were not only places of worship but also political statements, reinforcing Augustus' role as a pious leader who restored the favor of the gods upon Rome. These temples often commemorated important victories or symbolized Augustus' connection to divine authority, further legitimizing his rule in the eyes of the people.

Augustus also invested heavily in improving Rome's infrastructure, which directly benefited its citizens and demonstrated his commitment to their well-being. The construction and maintenance of roads, aqueducts, and public buildings were key components of this effort. Roads, in particular, were vital to the functioning of the Roman Empire, facilitating trade, military movements, and communication across vast distances. Augustus expanded the road network both in and around Rome, ensuring that the city was better connected to the provinces. His investment in roads not only boosted the economy but also symbolized the unity and reach of the Roman Empire under his leadership.

Aqueducts were another critical aspect of Augustus' infrastructure projects. Clean and accessible water was essential for the health and prosperity of Rome's population. Augustus oversaw the repair and extension of the city's aqueduct system, ensuring that water flowed to public baths, fountains, and private homes. The Aqua Virgo and Aqua Julia are just two examples of aqueducts that were either completed or renovated under his direction. These projects were tangible improvements that enhanced the quality of life for ordinary citizens, further endearing Augustus to the public.

Public buildings, such as the Forum of Augustus, were also central to his urban development plan. The Forum, adorned with statues of great Roman leaders and mythological figures, served as a symbol of Augustus' commitment to restoring the dignity and tradition of Rome. The grandeur of the Forum made it a center of political life, legal proceedings, and social gatherings, elevating Augustus' standing as a leader who brought prosperity and stability. These spaces weren't just functional—they were designed to inspire awe and reverence for Rome's greatness, with Augustus positioned at the heart of this renewed glory.

In addition to religious and civic structures, Augustus emphasized entertainment venues, such as theaters and amphitheaters, which were vital to Roman social life. He repaired the Theater of Pompey and completed the Theater of Marcellus, which provided spaces for public games and performances. These venues helped to reinforce his popularity among the people by offering spectacles that distracted from political tensions and provided a sense of normalcy and celebration. The ability to associate his reign with prosperity, peace, and entertainment was a key aspect of Augustus' public image.

By investing in these monumental projects, Augustus not only improved the physical state of Rome but also strengthened his personal legacy. The people of Rome saw the tangible benefits of his leadership in their everyday lives, from cleaner water and better roads to grander temples and public spaces. Each project was a statement of Augustus' power, generosity, and foresight, tying his name to the flourishing of the Roman state.

Through his public works, Augustus established himself as a ruler who cared deeply for the well-being of the Roman people. His investment in infrastructure projects improved the daily lives of his citizens while simultaneously creating lasting symbols of his authority. The transformation of Rome into a city of marble became a powerful narrative, ensuring that Augustus was remembered not just as a political leader but as a builder of a new Rome—one that embodied the stability, prosperity, and power of his reign.

Key Takeaway: Mastering the Art of Perception

AUGUSTUS' REIGN STANDS as one of the greatest examples in history of how mastering public perception is fundamental to maintaining and solidifying power. He understood that in the volatile environment of Roman politics, control over the narrative was as important as control over armies and legislation. By shaping how the public and the Senate perceived him, Augustus was able to quietly consolidate immense personal power while avoiding the fate of his predecessor, Julius Caesar, who openly pursued dictatorship and met a violent end.

Augustus realized that the key to securing lasting power lay in appearing to serve the Republic rather than dominate it. He crafted his public image as the "restorer of the Republic," positioning himself as a defender of Roman values and traditions rather than a tyrant. His relinquishment of extraordinary powers to the Senate, while symbolic, convinced the public and political elites that he was not seeking to usurp their authority. In truth, Augustus retained control over the military, key provinces, and political processes, yet his outward humility allowed him to navigate Roman society without sparking revolt or widespread opposition.

The success of Augustus' reign demonstrates that perception, when controlled effectively, can manipulate the very nature of governance. He was able to present his accumulation of absolute power as the natural and necessary outcome of restoring peace and stability to a fractured empire. His strategic use of art, literature, public monuments, and even coins helped to reinforce this image of a benevolent leader guided by Rome's best interests. Every public appearance, decision, and project was designed to convey that Augustus was a servant of Rome, not its master.

Public perception wasn't just about appearances for Augustus; it was deeply tied to legitimacy. By aligning himself with Roman religious traditions, using Virgil's *Aeneid* to claim divine ancestry through Aeneas, and undertaking grand public works projects to beautify and strengthen Rome, Augustus embedded himself into the cultural and moral fabric of the empire. His portrayal as a pious, moral leader who governed in favor of the people solidified his authority, making it almost impossible for critics or potential rivals to question his rule without appearing to attack Rome itself.

Furthermore, Augustus understood that perception was not static but needed to be managed continually. His image as a bringer of peace (Pax Romana) and prosperity was reinforced through the regular commissioning of public games, spectacles, and large-scale building projects. These acts not only improved the lives of the Roman populace but also served to constantly remind them of the benefits of his rule. His architectural and infrastructural legacy was designed to symbolize a Rome reborn under his guidance—a city that reflected the glory and stability of his leadership.

Through his careful manipulation of public perception, Augustus was able to navigate the dangerous waters of Roman politics, maintaining the support of both the people and the Senate while gradually eroding the very institutions of the Republic. His reign of over 40 years marked a period of unparalleled peace and stability, a testament to the power of image and narrative control.

The lessons from Augustus' reign are clear and enduring: mastering the art of perception is not simply an advantage in leadership, it is a necessity. Leaders who can shape how they are viewed by the public and key stakeholders can achieve a level of authority that is difficult to challenge. Control over perception allows leaders to gain trust, minimize opposition, and present even radical changes as natural and beneficial. Whether in politics, business, or any other sphere of influence, the ability to craft and control one's image is essential for achieving and maintaining power. Augustus' reign remains a timeless reminder that perception is, in many ways, reality, and those who master it will often find themselves in command of both.

Chapter 4: Divide and Rule — Managing Enemies and Rivals

In a politically volatile environment like ancient Rome, the key to securing and maintaining power often lies in how effectively one manages enemies and rivals. Augustus understood this better than anyone. Throughout his rise to power, he employed a strategy of divide and rule, pitting his opponents against each other, neutralizing threats through strategic alliances, and eliminating rivals when necessary. He knew that the path to ultimate control was not through direct confrontation with every enemy but by carefully manipulating the political landscape to weaken his adversaries, often using their own ambitions against them.

Rather than seeking to crush all opposition through brute force, Augustus mastered the art of dividing his enemies, ensuring that no single coalition could grow strong enough to threaten his position. This strategy allowed him to keep his rivals occupied with their own conflicts while he gradually consolidated power. Whether through calculated betrayals, exploiting internal divisions, or carefully selecting which rivals to eliminate and which to spare, Augustus built a political network that enabled him to dominate the Roman world.

This chapter explores how Augustus skillfully managed his enemies and rivals, transforming potential threats into opportunities to strengthen his control. His ability to manipulate divisions, control alliances, and create rivalries among his adversaries helped him rise to power without facing a unified front of opposition. In managing his enemies, Augustus ensured that the greatest threats to his rule often came from within his opponents' ranks, not his own.

Neutralizing Opposition

ONE OF THE MOST CRUCIAL aspects of Augustus' rise to power was his ability to neutralize opposition. He lived in a time of immense political instability, where rivals and enemies abounded, each vying for control of Rome. To secure his position and eliminate threats, Augustus employed a combination of strategic alliances, political maneuvering, and, most notably, the brutal use of proscription lists—an officially sanctioned practice of eliminating political enemies by labeling them as outlaws and confiscating their properties.

Following Julius Caesar's assassination in 44 BCE, the Roman Republic was in chaos. Augustus, then known as Octavian, was faced with powerful adversaries like Brutus and Cassius, leaders of the conspiracy to kill Caesar, as well as influential statesmen like Cicero, who initially opposed his rise. As Augustus sought to avenge Caesar's death and consolidate his power, he joined forces with Mark Antony and Lepidus in the Second Triumvirate, forming an alliance that allowed him to eliminate these key rivals.

One of the most notorious tools used by the Triumvirate to deal with opposition was the proscription list. Introduced in 43 BCE, this list allowed the triumvirs to declare certain individuals enemies of the state, effectively marking them for death. Proscribed individuals were stripped of their rights, their property was confiscated, and they could be executed with impunity by anyone. The use of proscription was both a practical and political move—it removed key political opponents while filling the coffers of the Triumvirate with the wealth of the proscribed.

Among the most prominent figures to fall victim to the proscriptions was Cicero, the famous orator and statesman. Cicero had been a vocal critic of Mark Antony and, by extension, a potential threat to Augustus' alliance with him. Although Cicero had initially supported Octavian's rise as a counterbalance to Antony's power, once

Octavian formed the Triumvirate, Cicero's fate was sealed. He was placed on the proscription list and subsequently hunted down and killed. Cicero's death sent a powerful message to others who might oppose the new order: no one, not even Rome's most famous orator, was safe from the Triumvirate's reach.

In addition to Cicero, Augustus targeted the leaders of Caesar's assassination, Brutus and Cassius. While the proscriptions were focused primarily on internal enemies within Rome, Augustus, alongside Antony, directed military efforts against Brutus and Cassius, who had fled to the eastern provinces to build armies in opposition to the Triumvirate. The conflict came to a head at the Battle of Philippi in 42 BCE, where the forces of Brutus and Cassius were decisively defeated. Both men committed suicide rather than be captured, eliminating two of the most prominent figures who could challenge Augustus' rise to power.

Augustus' use of proscriptions was not merely about eliminating immediate threats—it was also about consolidating control over Roman society. By targeting wealthy and influential individuals, the triumvirs could appropriate their estates, redistributing wealth to loyal supporters and replenishing their war funds. The proscriptions also served as a stark warning to anyone who might consider defying Augustus or his allies: opposition could lead to a swift and brutal death.

The proscriptions were not without controversy, however. While they were effective in eliminating rivals, they also created fear and resentment among the Roman elite, who were acutely aware that their wealth and lives could be at risk. Augustus was careful to distance himself from the worst excesses of the proscriptions once they had served their purpose, framing his later policies as restorative rather than punitive. As he transitioned from a figure of war to a figure of peace, Augustus worked to restore order and stability to Rome, presenting himself as a leader who had purged the state of its enemies in order to bring about a new era of prosperity.

Through the use of proscriptions, Augustus effectively neutralized political opposition, securing his path to power. This ruthless approach allowed him to eliminate key rivals while also securing the financial resources needed to support his growing power base. Though brutal, the proscription lists were a calculated move, showing Augustus' willingness to use extreme measures to protect his position and further his ultimate goal of becoming Rome's unchallenged leader.

Rivals Turned Allies

ONE OF THE HALLMARKS of Augustus' political strategy was his ability to use clemency as a tool to turn rivals into allies. Augustus understood that while ruthlessly eliminating opposition through proscriptions was necessary at times, there were situations where showing magnanimity could serve a greater purpose. By pardoning certain enemies, Augustus not only avoided alienating influential figures but also demonstrated his capacity for mercy, thereby strengthening his public image as a benevolent ruler who sought to unify Rome rather than destroy it.

Augustus' decision to offer clemency was often calculated and pragmatic, aimed at transforming potential threats into loyal supporters. This strategy allowed him to neutralize opposition without resorting to constant violence and ensured that influential rivals could be co-opted into his regime, thus avoiding prolonged resistance. By showing mercy when it suited him, Augustus could appear both strong and forgiving, projecting an image of a ruler who prioritized Rome's stability over personal vendettas.

One of the most famous examples of Augustus' use of clemency was his treatment of Marcus Aemilius Lepidus, his former ally in the Second Triumvirate. Lepidus, once a key figure alongside Augustus and Mark Antony, attempted to seize power for himself by launching a rebellion in Sicily after the defeat of Sextus Pompey. Rather than execute Lepidus, Augustus stripped him of his political and military power but allowed him to live out his days in comfortable exile. This decision demonstrated Augustus' ability to punish disloyalty while stopping short of creating a martyr. By sparing Lepidus, Augustus sent a message that disobedience would not be tolerated, but also that he was not eager to resort to bloodshed when unnecessary.

Another notable case of Augustus' calculated clemency was his relationship with Lucius Cornelius Balbus, an ally of Pompey and a former opponent of Julius Caesar. Instead of punishing Balbus for his past alliances, Augustus brought him into his inner circle. By forgiving Balbus and integrating him into his administration, Augustus gained the support of Balbus' influential network. This pardon not only expanded Augustus' political base but also showed that he was willing to set aside past enmities if it benefited Rome's future.

The clemency Augustus displayed toward many of Julius Caesar's assassins is another clear example of this strategy. While Brutus and Cassius, the ringleaders of the conspiracy, were ultimately defeated at Philippi, others involved in the assassination plot, such as Gaius Cassius Parmensis and others of lower rank, were spared or pardoned. By showing mercy to these figures, Augustus prevented the creation of a lasting legacy of vengeance, which could have further destabilized Rome. Instead, he chose to demonstrate that his leadership was one of reconciliation, signaling the end of internal conflict and the beginning of a new era of unity under his rule.

Clemency was not only used to win over former enemies but also to build Augustus' image as a compassionate and wise leader. In a society that valued honor and the concept of *clementia* (mercy), Augustus' calculated pardons resonated with the Roman elite and the public alike. It allowed him to contrast himself with the brutal proscriptions that marked the rule of previous leaders like Sulla, and even the Triumvirate's earlier years, reinforcing the idea that Augustus was different—someone who would lead Rome into a golden age rather than rule through fear and terror.

The political benefits of clemency also extended to Augustus' rivals who were too powerful to confront directly. For example, his eventual pardoning and inclusion of Marcus Agrippa, his former rival for power, into his inner circle, solidified Agrippa's loyalty and contributed to Augustus' military and political successes. Agrippa went on to serve as Augustus' closest ally and military commander, playing a vital role in securing victories like the Battle of Actium.

In sum, Augustus' use of clemency was a sophisticated political tool that allowed him to turn potential threats into valuable allies. It served to consolidate his power, weaken opposition without inciting further conflict, and enhance his image as a leader who sought to heal Rome's divisions rather than deepen them. By strategically pardoning rivals, Augustus was able to build a broad coalition of supporters, demonstrating that in the quest for long-term power, mercy could be just as effective as ruthlessness.

Mark Antony and Cleopatra

THE POLITICAL AND MILITARY rivalry between Augustus (then Octavian) and Mark Antony was one of the most significant power struggles in Roman history. It culminated in the decisive Battle of Actium in 31 BCE, but the roots of their conflict lay in the complex interplay of political maneuvering, personal rivalries, and Antony's increasingly controversial relationship with Cleopatra, the Queen of Egypt. Augustus, a master of political strategy and perception, used Antony's alliance with Cleopatra to systematically undermine his rival, both politically and morally, ultimately leading to Antony's downfall and Augustus' ascent to unrivaled power.

After forming the Second Triumvirate with Antony and Lepidus in 43 BCE, Augustus and Antony initially cooperated to eliminate their mutual enemies, including Julius Caesar's assassins, Brutus and Cassius. However, as the Triumvirate began to fracture, it became clear that the true struggle for control of Rome would be between Augustus and Antony. The division of the Roman world into spheres of influence—Antony ruling the eastern provinces and Augustus controlling the west—set the stage for inevitable conflict. Antony's decision to align himself with Cleopatra proved to be both a personal and political miscalculation, which Augustus deftly exploited.

Antony's relationship with Cleopatra, which began as a political alliance but soon became a deep personal affair, provided Augustus with the perfect weapon to discredit his rival. Cleopatra, as the ruler of Egypt, represented both wealth and influence, but she was also a foreign monarch, and many Romans viewed her with suspicion and disdain. Augustus, sensing an opportunity, began a campaign to depict Antony not as a Roman leader, but as a man who had abandoned his Roman identity and fallen under the control of a foreign queen.

The personal nature of Antony's relationship with Cleopatra only fueled Augustus' propaganda efforts. Antony fathered children with

Cleopatra and became more entwined with Egyptian politics, which alienated many in Rome. In 34 BCE, Antony held the *Donations of Alexandria* ceremony, where he publicly distributed Roman and eastern territories to Cleopatra and their children. This act was perceived in Rome as a betrayal of Roman interests and values, further damaging Antony's standing. Augustus seized on this event, portraying Antony as a man who had forsaken Rome and placed foreign interests, and his love for Cleopatra, above the needs of the Republic.

One of Augustus' most effective moves in this political chess game was his use of Antony's will. Augustus' agents managed to obtain a copy of Antony's will, which included provisions that Antony wanted to be buried in Alexandria, next to Cleopatra, rather than in Rome. Augustus made this public, exploiting Roman fears of foreign influence and betrayal. The revelation that Antony would forsake Roman burial traditions in favor of Cleopatra was a shocking affront to Roman pride and further convinced the Senate and people that Antony had abandoned his Roman identity in favor of Egypt and Cleopatra's ambitions.

Through careful manipulation of public opinion, Augustus positioned himself as the defender of Roman tradition and values, in stark contrast to Antony, whom he framed as a man corrupted by the exotic luxuries and influences of the East. Augustus did not attack Antony directly; instead, he declared war on Cleopatra in 32 BCE, making the conflict appear as a necessary defense of Roman interests against a foreign threat, rather than an internal civil war. By focusing the war on Cleopatra, Augustus cleverly avoided alienating Antony's supporters within Rome and the legions still loyal to him.

This move allowed Augustus to rally Rome behind him while isolating Antony. Many of Antony's former allies were reluctant to support what they saw as a war fought on behalf of a foreign queen, and some defected to Augustus. The political and moral framing of the conflict played directly into Augustus' hands, weakening Antony's position both militarily and politically.

The final military confrontation came at the Battle of Actium in 31 BCE. Antony and Cleopatra's combined forces, including their powerful naval fleet, faced off against Augustus' forces, commanded by his close ally Agrippa. Augustus had successfully isolated Antony both diplomatically and militarily, and Agrippa's superior naval tactics led to a decisive victory. Antony and Cleopatra fled to Egypt, where they ultimately took their own lives, marking the end of their political and personal alliance.

Augustus' victory at Actium was more than just a military triumph—it was the culmination of years of political strategy, propaganda, and careful manipulation of Antony's vulnerabilities. By exploiting Antony's relationship with Cleopatra, Augustus had not only defeated his greatest rival but had also positioned himself as the savior of Rome. The defeat of Antony and Cleopatra allowed Augustus to consolidate power without facing further significant opposition, paving the way for his transformation into Rome's first emperor.

In the end, Augustus capitalized on Antony's personal entanglements with Cleopatra to frame him as a man who had betrayed Rome for the sake of a foreign queen. By focusing on Antony's moral and political failings, rather than simply relying on military force, Augustus was able to undermine his rival's reputation and legitimacy, turning Rome against him. This combination of propaganda, political maneuvering, and military prowess ensured that when Augustus emerged victorious, he did so with the full support of Rome behind him, securing his place as the undisputed leader of the Roman Empire.

Key Takeaway: The Balance Between Ruthlessness and Mercy

AUGUSTUS' RISE TO POWER and his reign as the first Roman emperor were marked by a careful balancing act between ruthlessness and mercy. This delicate combination allowed him to eliminate political rivals, maintain control, and secure stability without inciting widespread rebellion or creating a legacy of martyrs who could inspire future resistance. His ability to wield power with both severity and clemency was one of the key reasons for his long and successful reign, as it enabled him to neutralize threats without generating the resentment or unrest that so often accompanies oppressive rule. This chapter explores how Augustus managed this balance, using both calculated ruthlessness and strategic mercy to secure his hold on Rome.

The Early Ruthlessness: Proscriptions and the Consolidation of Power

In the early years of his political career, Augustus (then Octavian) was no stranger to ruthless methods. The proscriptions of 43 BCE, initiated during his alliance with Mark Antony and Lepidus in the Second Triumvirate, were one of the most brutal examples of political purges in Roman history. Proscriptions were public lists of individuals deemed enemies of the state, marking them for execution and the confiscation of their property. The proscriptions targeted not only those who had supported Julius Caesar's assassins, but also wealthy individuals whose wealth could be seized to fund the Triumvirate's military campaigns.

One of the most famous victims of the proscriptions was Cicero, the renowned orator and statesman. Cicero had been a vocal critic of Mark Antony and had initially supported Octavian as a counterbalance to Antony's power. However, once the Triumvirate was formed, Cicero found himself on the wrong side of political alliances. His execution was a clear example of the Triumvirate's willingness to eliminate even the most respected figures in Rome to secure their control.

The proscriptions were a tool of sheer ruthlessness. They allowed Augustus and his allies to remove key political opponents while also replenishing their war funds through the confiscation of assets. In this early phase of his career, Augustus demonstrated that he was willing to resort to extreme measures to eliminate threats and consolidate his position. However, it is important to note that while the proscriptions were a brutal method of control, they were largely carried out under the auspices of the Triumvirate, allowing Augustus to distance himself from their worst excesses as he later transitioned into a more merciful and stabilizing ruler.

Mercy as a Political Tool: Pardoning Rivals

As Augustus solidified his position as the dominant figure in Roman politics, he began to shift his approach from one of pure ruthlessness to a more calculated use of mercy. This change was not driven by a moral transformation, but rather by a recognition that mercy, when used strategically, could serve his long-term interests better than continued violence and purges.

One of the clearest examples of Augustus' calculated use of mercy was his treatment of Marcus Aemilius Lepidus, the third member of the Second Triumvirate. After Lepidus attempted to seize control of Sicily in 36 BCE, Augustus had every reason to eliminate him as a political rival. Instead, Augustus chose to strip Lepidus of his political power but allowed him to live out his days in comfortable exile. This decision was a shrewd one—it removed Lepidus as a threat without creating a new martyr for potential opposition to rally around. Augustus demonstrated that mercy could be just as effective as ruthlessness in neutralizing threats, particularly when it avoided unnecessary bloodshed and public outcry.

Augustus also used clemency to win over former enemies and rivals, such as Lucius Cornelius Balbus and other figures who had previously opposed Julius Caesar or the Triumvirate. Rather than executing or exiling all of his political enemies, Augustus selectively pardoned those who could serve his interests, co-opting them into his regime and expanding his political base. This strategy allowed him to appear magnanimous and conciliatory while strengthening his control by turning former adversaries into loyal allies. Mercy, in this context, became a tool of political consolidation, helping Augustus build a broader coalition of support.

By pardoning certain individuals, Augustus was able to present himself as a ruler who prioritized the unity and stability of Rome over personal vendettas. This image of clemency helped to distance him from the bloodshed of the proscriptions and the civil wars, positioning him as a leader focused on peace and reconciliation. Augustus was careful to select his moments of mercy strategically, ensuring that they always served his long-term goals.

Avoiding Martyrdom: The Death of Antony and Cleopatra

The handling of Mark Antony and Cleopatra's defeat is another example of Augustus' mastery in balancing ruthlessness with mercy. As his most formidable rival, Antony was a major threat to Augustus' ambition to become the sole ruler of Rome. Yet Augustus recognized that openly executing Antony could turn him into a martyr for his supporters, particularly those loyal to Antony's cause in the eastern provinces.

Instead of capturing Antony and publicly executing him, Augustus allowed events to unfold in a way that led to Antony's suicide after the defeat at the Battle of Actium in 31 BCE. By allowing Antony to take his own life, Augustus avoided the potential fallout of creating a martyr. Antony's death was perceived as the result of personal failure and despair rather than a political execution, which diminished any chance that he would become a symbol of resistance to Augustus' rule.

Cleopatra, too, was allowed to take her own life, though Augustus had originally planned to bring her back to Rome as a captive in a triumph. Her suicide, like Antony's, was a strategic boon for Augustus, as it eliminated the need for a public spectacle that could have rallied sympathy for her. With both Antony and Cleopatra dead by their own hands, Augustus had removed the last significant threat to his power without creating new martyrs or stirring up prolonged resistance from their supporters.

Maintaining Control Without Stirring Rebellion

Throughout his reign, Augustus continued to employ a combination of calculated ruthlessness and political mercy. When necessary, he acted decisively to eliminate threats, such as in his early use of the proscriptions and in his eventual defeat of Antony. However, he also understood that unrelenting brutality would only breed further resistance. By selectively offering clemency to rivals, pardoning enemies, and allowing some opponents to fade into obscurity rather than facing violent retribution, Augustus ensured that he did not provoke widespread rebellion.

A crucial aspect of Augustus' ability to maintain control without stirring up resistance was his careful management of public perception. By presenting himself as a ruler focused on restoring peace and stability, he was able to distance himself from the violence of the past and present his rule as one of benevolence. Augustus' mercy was always strategic, designed to enhance his image as a unifier and a restorer of Rome's glory. This perception allowed him to wield power with a light touch, neutralizing opposition while maintaining broad support among the Roman people.

Moreover, Augustus' careful use of mercy helped to maintain the illusion of Republican values. By avoiding the outright execution of political figures and focusing on peaceful reconciliation, he could claim that he was preserving Roman traditions, even as he concentrated unprecedented power in his own hands. This approach minimized the likelihood of organized resistance to his rule, as it appeared that

Augustus was working within the established system, rather than dismantling it outright.

Long-Term Stability Through the Balance of Ruthlessness and Mercy

In the long run, Augustus' careful balance of ruthlessness and mercy was key to the stability of his reign. He understood that securing power through fear and violence alone would lead to constant challenges and uprisings. By tempering ruthlessness with clemency, he was able to build a stable foundation for his rule, winning the loyalty of former rivals and presenting himself as a leader who prioritized the well-being of Rome over personal grudges.

This balance allowed Augustus to maintain control for over four decades, during which time Rome experienced relative peace and prosperity under what came to be known as the Pax Romana. Augustus' ability to avoid creating martyrs or stirring up resistance through excessive brutality contributed significantly to this period of stability. His strategic use of both mercy and ruthlessness not only secured his own power but also laid the groundwork for the long-term survival of the Roman Empire.

Conclusion

Augustus' mastery in balancing ruthlessness with mercy was a defining feature of his leadership. He was willing to eliminate threats when necessary, but he did so in a way that avoided creating martyrs or provoking further resistance. By offering clemency to certain rivals and using mercy as a political tool, Augustus was able to consolidate power, maintain stability, and secure his position as Rome's first emperor. His reign demonstrates that effective leadership often requires a careful mix of severity and forgiveness, ensuring that threats are neutralized without alienating potential supporters or creating new enemies. This balance allowed Augustus to build a legacy of long-term stability and peace that endured for centuries.

Chapter 5: Legal Manipulation — Using Laws to Consolidate Power

The rise of Augustus to become Rome's first emperor was not just a result of military victories or political alliances; it was deeply rooted in his ability to manipulate the law to serve his long-term objectives. In a society where tradition and legal precedent were highly valued, Augustus understood that power could not simply be seized—it had to be legitimized. His brilliance lay in his capacity to use existing laws and institutions, not to dismantle the Roman Republic outright, but to gradually reshape it into a system where he held ultimate control.

Augustus' mastery of legal manipulation allowed him to create the illusion of continuity with the Republic's past while systematically consolidating his own power. Rather than abolishing the Senate, eliminating the magistrates, or openly declaring himself king, he worked within the legal frameworks that had governed Rome for centuries, modifying them to serve his purposes. By doing so, he was able to present himself as the protector of Rome's traditions and values, all while shifting the real power away from the traditional Republican institutions and into his own hands.

This chapter explores how Augustus used the law as both a shield and a sword—shielding himself from the appearance of tyranny by working within the system, while simultaneously using legal reforms and precedents to carve out a new political structure centered around his authority. Augustus' strategic use of legal manipulation didn't just secure his position during his lifetime; it laid the foundation for a new form of government that would endure for centuries, with Roman emperors wielding vast power under the guise of Republican tradition.

Mastering the Senate

ONE OF AUGUSTUS' MOST masterful political achievements was his ability to manipulate the Roman Senate, transforming it from the heart of Republican governance into a rubber stamp for his policies while maintaining the illusion of its continued relevance and authority. Augustus understood that outright dissolving or openly marginalizing the Senate would spark resistance from Rome's elite, who were deeply invested in the Republican traditions that had defined Roman political life for centuries. Instead, Augustus employed a more subtle approach—he preserved the external structure and customs of the Senate but gradually hollowed out its power, concentrating authority in his own hands.

The foundation of Augustus' strategy lay in his careful positioning as a restorer of the Republic rather than a dictator. After his victory over Mark Antony and Cleopatra in 31 BCE, Augustus presented himself as a leader who sought to restore order and stability after years of civil war. In a highly publicized gesture of humility in 27 BCE, Augustus "returned" his extraordinary powers to the Senate and the Roman people, claiming that the Republic had been restored. This act, known as the *First Settlement*, was a carefully orchestrated political maneuver designed to win the support of the Senate and Roman elite, while in reality, it cemented Augustus' control.

Although Augustus appeared to relinquish power, the Senate, in gratitude for his supposed magnanimity, granted him a range of extraordinary titles and honors, including the title *Princeps* (first citizen), which allowed him to retain de facto control over Rome. Augustus was also granted imperium over key provinces, including those with the most important military legions, ensuring that he maintained command over Rome's military forces. Thus, while the Senate continued to meet and deliberate, it was Augustus who truly held the reins of power.

To further solidify his control, Augustus carefully curated the membership of the Senate, purging it of those who opposed him and filling its ranks with loyal supporters. He conducted multiple purges and reforms of the Senate, reducing its size and ensuring that it was populated by individuals who were either indebted to him or sympathetic to his vision for Rome. This gradual reshaping of the Senate allowed Augustus to ensure that his policies were passed without significant resistance, as the Senate was filled with men who were either loyal to him or who had a vested interest in maintaining the status quo that Augustus had established.

Despite this manipulation, Augustus was careful to maintain the appearance of Republican governance. He allowed the Senate to debate and vote on matters, but these were often matters of little consequence, with Augustus controlling the most important decisions behind the scenes. He maintained the facade that the Senate remained an independent body with the authority to govern Rome, even as he steadily accumulated the real levers of power. By doing so, Augustus avoided alienating the senatorial class, allowing them to retain their sense of dignity and influence, even as their actual political power waned.

Another key aspect of Augustus' manipulation of the Senate was his use of propaganda and public perception. Through monumental architecture, literature, and public spectacles, Augustus portrayed himself as a humble servant of the Republic, emphasizing that his rule was a continuation of traditional Roman values. This narrative helped to placate the Senate and the Roman elite, who could view Augustus not as a tyrant but as a stabilizing force who respected the Republic's institutions. Augustus' careful control of his image allowed him to rule as an autocrat without appearing to have dismantled the Republican system.

Augustus also understood that the illusion of shared power would help prevent unrest. By preserving the Senate's ceremonial and consultative roles, he gave Rome's elite a sense of participation in governance, even though the ultimate authority rested with him. This careful balance allowed Augustus to avoid the appearance of dictatorship, instead creating a system that functioned as an empire in all but name. The Senate, though largely ceremonial under Augustus, was still an important institution in maintaining the stability of his regime by giving legitimacy to his decisions.

Over time, Augustus' manipulation of the Senate became so effective that it ceased to be a meaningful check on his power. The Senate's role became increasingly symbolic, providing a veneer of traditional Republican governance while Augustus controlled the most critical aspects of political, military, and economic power. The Senate continued to exist, but it was Augustus who directed the future of the Roman Empire, making decisions that the Senate largely approved without question.

The brilliance of Augustus' manipulation of the Senate lay in his ability to maintain the illusion of Republican governance. By respecting the forms and traditions of the Senate, he avoided the fate of Julius Caesar, whose open ambition for absolute power had led to his assassination. Augustus, on the other hand, created a system in which the Senate appeared to govern, but in reality, he wielded the true authority. This subtle yet effective control allowed Augustus to reign for decades without facing significant opposition from the Senate or the broader Roman elite.

In conclusion, Augustus' mastery of the Senate was a key aspect of his long-term success. By turning the Senate into a compliant body while maintaining the outward appearance of Republican governance, he was able to consolidate power without sparking widespread resistance. His manipulation of the Senate allowed him to secure legitimacy, avoid the dangers of autocratic rule, and create a stable political system that would endure for centuries. This ability to balance

tradition with realpolitik was one of the defining features of Augustus'
reign, marking him as a master of political strategy and perception.

Augustus' Reforms

AS AUGUSTUS CONSOLIDATED his power and transitioned Rome from a Republic to an Empire, his reign was marked by a series of key legal reforms that helped stabilize the state and centralize authority under his leadership. Recognizing that Rome's political and social fabric had been weakened by decades of civil war, Augustus aimed to restore order, enforce moral behavior, and create a more cohesive society that could support his vision of a stable and prosperous empire. These reforms, which touched nearly every aspect of Roman life, were designed not only to maintain control over the sprawling empire but also to present Augustus as a moral and righteous ruler who was restoring Rome's traditional values.

One of the most significant sets of legal reforms enacted by Augustus was the *lex Julia*, a series of laws that regulated public morality, family life, and citizenship. These laws served multiple purposes: they enforced social order, promoted the traditional Roman values that Augustus wanted to be associated with, and helped solidify his role as the moral leader of Rome.

The *Lex Julia* on Morality and Family Life

The *lex Julia de maritandis ordinibus* (Julian Law on Marriage and Social Orders), introduced in 18 BCE, was designed to encourage marriage and childbearing, particularly among the Roman elite. Augustus was concerned about the declining birthrate among the upper classes, which he saw as a threat to Rome's future. The law mandated that members of the senatorial and equestrian classes marry and produce legitimate children, reinforcing the importance of the family unit as the foundation of Roman society. By incentivizing marriage and family life, Augustus hoped to ensure the continuation of Rome's ruling class, which he believed was necessary for the stability and governance of the empire.

In addition to encouraging marriage, the *lex Julia* imposed penalties on those who remained unmarried or childless after a certain age. Men who did not marry by the age of 25 and women who did not marry by 20 faced social and financial consequences, such as restrictions on inheriting property. By attaching penalties to failure to marry, Augustus was effectively using the law to enforce traditional Roman values and encourage the kind of social behavior that would support a stable and orderly society.

Another aspect of the *lex Julia* was the *lex Julia de adulteriis coercendis* (Julian Law on Adultery), which was enacted in 17 BCE to combat what Augustus perceived as the growing moral decay in Roman society. This law criminalized adultery and made it a public offense, punishable by exile, fines, or death in severe cases. Adultery was seen not just as a private matter but as a crime against the family and, by extension, the state. Augustus' crackdown on adultery was part of his broader effort to enforce moral discipline, reinforcing the idea that Roman citizens should uphold traditional family values and the sanctity of marriage.

This focus on morality was not purely about restoring traditional values; it was also a political tool. By positioning himself as the enforcer of morality, Augustus could present himself as a stabilizing figure who was bringing order and virtue back to a society that had been fractured by years of civil conflict. His moral reforms were intended to cultivate an image of Augustus as a ruler who cared deeply about the health and future of Roman society, further legitimizing his rule.

The *Lex Julia* on Governance and Public Behavior

Beyond personal morality, the *lex Julia* also encompassed laws that regulated public behavior and governance. These reforms were designed to centralize power, maintain public order, and reinforce Augustus' control over the various institutions of the state.

The *lex Julia municipalis* was a set of regulations aimed at improving the administration of Rome's municipalities and local governance. This law outlined the responsibilities of local magistrates and officials, ensuring that local governments were more efficient and accountable. By standardizing the administration of Rome's cities and towns, Augustus strengthened the central government's control over the vast territories of the empire, making it easier to govern and maintain order.

Another key reform was the reorganization of the Roman legal system itself. Augustus reformed the judicial process to ensure that courts were more efficient and less corrupt. He appointed trusted magistrates and established new courts to handle specific types of cases, such as those involving the imperial family or matters of public interest. These reforms made the legal system more effective in administering justice, and by appointing loyal officials to key positions, Augustus ensured that the judiciary remained firmly under his control.

Furthermore, Augustus implemented financial reforms, creating a more centralized and transparent system for tax collection. One of the most significant steps in this area was the creation of the *aerarium militare*, a military treasury established in 6 CE to provide for the payment of soldiers' pensions. By setting aside funds specifically for veterans, Augustus strengthened the loyalty of the military, ensuring that they remained a reliable and well-supported force under his command. This reform also reduced the burden on individual commanders, who had previously been responsible for rewarding their soldiers, further centralizing control over the military under Augustus' authority.

Moral Legislation as Political Strategy

While Augustus' moral legislation served to reinforce traditional Roman values, these reforms were also a critical part of his broader political strategy. Augustus was acutely aware that his position as the first Roman emperor required more than just military might or legal authority—it required the support of the Roman people and the perception that his rule was a return to order and stability after the chaos of the late Republic. By framing his reforms as a moral and social restoration, Augustus was able to strengthen his image as a righteous and paternal figure who was looking out for the well-being of the Roman state.

One of the most significant consequences of Augustus' moral reforms was the way they linked the health of the state to the moral behavior of its citizens. By positioning himself as the defender of Roman virtue, Augustus created a direct connection between his personal authority and the well-being of the empire. The success of his moral reforms became intertwined with the success of his reign, making it difficult for opponents to challenge his authority without also appearing to challenge the stability and morality of Rome itself.

The Long-Term Impact of Augustus' Reforms

Augustus' legal reforms had a profound and lasting impact on Rome. His efforts to restore moral order, strengthen family values, and centralize governance created a more stable and cohesive society that could support the empire's expansion and longevity. By enforcing laws that regulated both public and private behavior, Augustus helped to shape a Roman culture that valued discipline, loyalty, and order—values that would become central to the identity of the Roman Empire.

Moreover, Augustus' legal reforms set a precedent for future emperors, who would continue to use laws and moral legislation to reinforce their own authority. The balance between centralizing power and maintaining the appearance of a traditional Roman Republic allowed Augustus to create a stable political system that endured for centuries.

In conclusion, Augustus' legal reforms were a cornerstone of his efforts to stabilize and centralize power in Rome. Through the *lex Julia* and other key laws, he was able to regulate public and private behavior, promote traditional Roman values, and create a more efficient system of governance. These reforms not only strengthened Augustus' control over the Roman state but also helped to establish the foundation for the long-term success of the Roman Empire. By combining moral authority with legal power, Augustus ensured that his reign would be remembered not just for military conquests but for the lasting stability he brought to Rome.

Cementing Authority through Legal Precedent

ONE OF AUGUSTUS' MOST effective strategies for consolidating his power was his use of existing Roman laws and legal precedents to legitimize his authority while quietly stripping power from the traditional Republican institutions, like the Senate and popular assemblies. By anchoring his reforms and actions in established Roman legal traditions, Augustus maintained the appearance of respect for Republican values, even as he centralized power in his hands. This subtle approach allowed him to present himself as a restorer of Roman tradition, not a dictator, while fundamentally transforming the nature of Roman governance into a de facto autocracy.

The Illusion of Republican Restoration

When Augustus first took control after his victory over Mark Antony and Cleopatra, he recognized that the Roman people, especially the senatorial elite, still valued the idea of the Republic. They had long been resistant to the idea of a sole ruler or king. Augustus, therefore, carefully avoided the appearance of openly dismantling Republican institutions. Instead, he worked within the system, using legal precedents and existing structures to strengthen his personal authority.

The turning point came in 27 BCE, when Augustus, in a calculated move, "returned" his powers to the Senate and the Roman people in a public ceremony known as the *First Settlement*. This act was framed as a renunciation of his extraordinary powers and a return to the Republican order. In response, the Senate, grateful for his magnanimity, bestowed upon him a series of honors and new titles, most notably *Princeps* (first citizen) and *Imperator* (commander), granting him effective control over the military and key provinces.

Augustus' ability to use this moment to cement his authority was critical. By cloaking his dominance in the language of Republican restoration, he avoided the fate of Julius Caesar, whose open assumption of power had led to his assassination. Augustus used the *First Settlement* to create the appearance of a shared governance system while securing for himself the most important military and political powers. This allowed him to hold real authority without openly challenging Republican ideals, all while carefully maintaining the pretense that Rome was still a functioning Republic.

The Use of *Imperium* and Proconsular Power

A key element of Augustus' strategy was his use of *imperium* (the legal authority to command) and proconsular power to legitimize his control over Rome's military and provinces. After the *First Settlement*, Augustus was granted *imperium proconsulare maius*, which gave him authority over all of Rome's provinces with military forces, particularly the strategically important regions like Egypt, Gaul, and Hispania. This power effectively placed Rome's legions under his direct control, making Augustus the de facto military leader of the empire.

This grant of power was not unprecedented in Roman history—generals during the Republic had often been given temporary command over specific provinces during times of war. However, Augustus' use of *imperium proconsulare maius* was different because it was neither temporary nor limited. By securing command over the provinces with the most military resources, Augustus ensured that he alone controlled the empire's military power, while the Senate and traditional Republican institutions were left to govern more peaceful, administrative provinces.

By presenting this authority as part of a legal precedent rooted in Republican traditions, Augustus could justify his control without appearing to subvert the system. The Senate retained the illusion of power over certain territories, but the reality was that Augustus' military supremacy ensured his unchallenged authority.

Consolidating Judicial Power

Augustus also consolidated his authority by reforming the Roman judicial system, effectively centralizing legal power under his control.

He maintained the existing framework of Roman law but introduced key changes that allowed him to exercise influence over judicial outcomes. By appointing loyal magistrates and judges to key positions, Augustus ensured that his legal reforms and decisions would be carried out in ways that benefited his regime.

For example, Augustus established new courts to handle specific types of cases, particularly those related to public morality, as part of his broader moral reform agenda. These courts were often staffed by officials loyal to Augustus, ensuring that cases were decided in ways that aligned with his vision for Roman society. Through these judicial reforms, Augustus not only centralized legal authority but also reinforced his image as a moral leader who was restoring order and discipline to Rome after years of civil war and chaos.

In addition, Augustus had the power to convene the Senate and introduce legislation, which allowed him to shape the legal and legislative agenda of the empire. While the Senate technically retained the right to pass laws, it was Augustus who proposed and often drafted key legislation, ensuring that his policies were enacted without opposition. This created the impression that the Senate was still a functioning legislative body, even as it increasingly became a tool for Augustus to rubber-stamp his decisions.

The *Lex Julia* and Moral Legislation

Augustus used legal precedent not only to consolidate political power but also to present himself as the moral and cultural guardian of Rome. Through the *lex Julia*, a series of laws that regulated public morality, family life, and citizenship, Augustus positioned himself as the protector of traditional Roman values. These laws, which included provisions on marriage, adultery, and public behavior, reinforced his authority by linking his leadership to the moral health of the empire.

The *lex Julia* built on long-standing Roman traditions of social discipline and family values, but Augustus expanded these laws to serve his broader political goals. By associating his reign with the enforcement of morality, Augustus was able to frame his control over society as a necessary restoration of Rome's moral and civic foundations, further legitimizing his rule.

These moral reforms also allowed Augustus to reinforce the importance of the family unit and the continuity of the elite ruling class, which supported his regime. By positioning himself as the champion of Roman morality, Augustus created a lasting legacy that tied his leadership to the health and stability of Roman society. These laws not only strengthened his authority but also created a social framework that future emperors would follow.

The Gradual Erosion of Traditional Institutions

While Augustus used legal precedent to legitimize his authority, he simultaneously stripped traditional Republican institutions of real power. The Senate, which had once been the central body of governance, was reduced to a largely ceremonial role. Augustus maintained the outward appearance of a functioning Senate, allowing it to meet and deliberate on certain matters, but the most important decisions—particularly those related to military and foreign policy—were controlled by Augustus alone.

By filling the Senate with loyal supporters and maintaining the facade of Republican governance, Augustus ensured that the Senate continued to function as a rubber stamp for his policies. He carefully managed Senate appointments and purges, removing political opponents and promoting individuals who were loyal to his regime. Over time, the Senate became less of an independent governing body and more of a formal institution that provided legitimacy to Augustus' decisions.

Augustus also maintained the traditional offices of the Republic, such as the consulship and the tribunate, but he often held these positions himself or controlled who was appointed to them. By holding the consulship and later the tribunician power, Augustus secured control over the legislative process and the ability to veto any laws or decisions that did not align with his agenda. These offices, while technically part of the Republican system, became tools of Augustus' autocratic control.

The Creation of the Principate

By working within the existing legal framework and using established Roman laws and customs, Augustus was able to create a new form of government: the Principate. This system maintained the outward appearance of the Roman Republic, with its Senate and magistrates, but concentrated real power in the hands of one individual. Augustus was able to present himself as a restorer of the Republic, while in reality, he had established a new form of monarchy that would endure for centuries.

The Principate allowed Augustus to avoid the pitfalls that had led to the downfall of previous leaders like Julius Caesar, whose open pursuit of power had triggered backlash and assassination. By grounding his authority in legal precedent and working within the traditional framework of Roman governance, Augustus ensured that his reign was viewed as legitimate, even as he systematically dismantled the old Republican structures.

Conclusion

Augustus' ability to use existing laws and legal precedents to cement his authority was one of the most remarkable aspects of his political strategy. By maintaining the outward forms of Republican governance while centralizing power in his own hands, he was able to legitimize his rule and avoid the appearance of dictatorship. Augustus' use of legal reforms, particularly the *lex Julia* and the manipulation of traditional offices and the Senate, allowed him to consolidate power without provoking widespread resistance from Rome's elite. Through these legal precedents, Augustus not only secured his own position as the first Roman emperor but also laid the foundation for the imperial system that would dominate Roman politics for centuries.

Key Takeaway: The Power of Legal Manipulation—Using Law Not Just for Governance, But as a Means of Solidifying Long-Term Control

THE GENIUS OF AUGUSTUS' reign lay in his deep understanding of the law, not just as a tool for governance but as a powerful instrument to secure and legitimize his control. Throughout his rise and rule, Augustus skillfully manipulated legal structures to consolidate his power while maintaining the illusion of Republican traditions. Rather than imposing himself as a dictator, he used the legal framework of Rome to weave his authority into the very fabric of the state, ensuring that his rule would be both stable and enduring.

Augustus' legal strategy began with the *First Settlement* of 27 BCE, where he masterfully staged a public renunciation of his extraordinary powers, only to have the Senate restore them in a more permanent form. By returning power "to the people and Senate," Augustus created the illusion of humility and Republican virtue. However, in reality, this maneuver allowed him to maintain control over the military and key provinces, including the critical frontier territories where Rome's legions were stationed. This was a legal manipulation of the highest order—using a symbolic gesture of Republican restoration to mask the consolidation of unprecedented personal power. It set the stage for Augustus' long rule and became a model for future emperors, who would similarly cloak their autocratic authority in the appearance of traditional Roman governance.

The brilliance of Augustus' approach was that he never needed to outwardly dismantle the institutions of the Republic. The Senate still convened, magistrates were still appointed, and laws were still debated. However, Augustus controlled all meaningful decisions, often by holding titles such as Princeps (first citizen), Imperator (commander), and later, the tribunician power, which gave him the right to introduce and veto laws at will. The Senate, though appearing to function as it always had, gradually became a body that rubber-stamped Augustus' policies. By maintaining the structure of the Republic, Augustus avoided the backlash that would have arisen had he overtly declared himself a monarch. Instead, he used existing laws and titles to weave his power into the traditional system, allowing him to rule as an emperor in all but name.

In addition to his political maneuvering, Augustus used legal reforms to shape Roman society and align it with his broader goals of stability and moral order. The lex Julia, a series of laws regulating marriage, adultery, and public morality, was one of his most famous legal innovations. These laws sought to revive traditional Roman values, encouraging marriage and childbearing while penalizing adultery and celibacy. While ostensibly about restoring moral virtue, these laws served a deeper purpose: they reinforced Augustus' image as the moral custodian of Rome. By associating his reign with the health and virtue of Roman society, Augustus further legitimized his rule, making it clear that his authority was not just political but moral.

The lex Julia was also a way for Augustus to shape Rome's elite. By imposing penalties on childless elites and encouraging marriage among the upper classes, Augustus ensured that Rome's ruling families would remain stable and produce heirs to carry on the governance of the empire. This legal manipulation ensured the continuity of Rome's political class, but it also reinforced Augustus' control over the social order. By using law to govern personal behavior, Augustus extended his reach into the private lives of Rome's most powerful citizens, making them dependent on his approval and governance.

Furthermore, Augustus reformed the judicial and financial systems to reinforce his authority. He created new courts and appointed loyal magistrates to handle legal matters, especially cases of public interest and those involving moral violations. These reforms ensured that legal disputes would be settled in ways that aligned with Augustus' broader goals, and that justice would be administered by individuals loyal to him. Augustus also established the *aerarium militare*, a military treasury that provided pensions for retired soldiers, which not only secured the loyalty of the military but also centralized financial control under his administration. By tying the economic well-being of Rome's soldiers and citizens to his rule, Augustus further ensured that his position would remain secure.

Through his legal reforms, Augustus was able to strip power from traditional Republican institutions, such as the Senate and popular assemblies, while preserving their outward forms. He did not abolish these bodies outright but made them functionally irrelevant by ensuring that all real power resided with him. His reforms allowed him to control every aspect of Roman governance, from the military and legal systems to financial and moral oversight. The brilliance of Augustus' approach was that by working within the existing legal framework, he avoided the need for violent upheaval or drastic changes that would have alienated Rome's elite or the general population. Instead, he gradually shifted the locus of power to himself, using law as a tool for long-term control.

In many ways, Augustus' ability to manipulate the law set the precedent for Roman emperors who followed. The Principate that he established—a system where the emperor held ultimate power but operated within the veneer of Republican institutions—would endure for centuries. Future emperors would continue to use the law as a means of solidifying their control, working within the structures Augustus had redefined to govern an empire that stretched across vast territories and diverse peoples.

The key lesson from Augustus' reign is that law, when used strategically, is not just a mechanism for governance. It can be a tool for embedding power so deeply into the fabric of the state that it becomes virtually unassailable. By controlling the legal framework, Augustus ensured that his rule was seen as legitimate, both in his time and in the eyes of history. His manipulation of the law allowed him to create a system that could function long after his death, ensuring the stability and continuity of the Roman Empire. In the end, Augustus' legacy was not just about military conquest or political cunning—it was about his ability to use the law as a weapon of governance, transforming Rome into an empire that would last for centuries.

Chapter 6: Soft Power — Winning the Hearts of the People

Augustus' reign was a masterclass in balancing power, not just through military might but by cultivating a deep connection with the Roman people. While his military victories against enemies like Mark Antony and Cleopatra solidified his control over Rome, he recognized that true, long-term stability required more than just the sword. To maintain his authority, Augustus knew he had to foster loyalty, trust, and even admiration from the very citizens who had experienced decades of civil unrest and political instability. His strategy for winning and keeping the hearts of the Roman people is what we now understand as soft power.

Soft power—winning influence and securing loyalty through attraction rather than coercion—became central to Augustus' rule. Through public works projects, generous distributions of food, spectacular games, and moral reforms, Augustus presented himself not just as a military leader but as a paternal figure devoted to the well-being of his people. By doing so, he carefully balanced his role as an autocrat with the image of a benefactor, ensuring that the people saw him as indispensable to Rome's prosperity and peace.

Public works, from roads and aqueducts to temples and forums, were visible symbols of Augustus' care for Rome and its citizens. These projects not only beautified the city but also provided jobs and improved living conditions, solidifying his connection with the urban poor. Similarly, the *annona*, the system of grain distribution, was a lifeline for many Roman citizens and reinforced the perception that

Augustus provided for their basic needs. By ensuring a steady supply of food and other necessities, he kept the people content, diverting their attention from political matters and maintaining their loyalty.

Entertainment was another tool Augustus used to secure popular favor. The public games he sponsored—gladiatorial contests, chariot races, and theatrical performances—weren't just distractions; they were a way to foster civic pride and collective joy. By personally sponsoring these events, Augustus made himself a central figure in the daily lives of Roman citizens, a leader who gave them pleasure and entertainment, not just laws and decrees.

Beyond the material and physical, Augustus worked to win the moral support of his people. His social and legal reforms promoted traditional Roman values such as family loyalty, marriage, and public morality. In this way, Augustus positioned himself as the moral leader of Rome, restoring not only political stability but also the ethical foundation of the empire. By aligning his rule with Rome's most cherished virtues, Augustus deepened his connection with the populace, building a base of support that transcended political affiliations.

In crafting this bond, Augustus ensured that his power was grounded not just in military strength or political maneuvering, but in the hearts and minds of his people. He understood that a content and loyal populace would be less likely to challenge his authority, allowing him to reshape Rome's government while maintaining the appearance of a Republic. This strategic use of soft power allowed Augustus to rule not just with authority, but with widespread public approval—a key factor in his ability to remain in power for over four decades.

Winning the hearts of the people wasn't just about securing loyalty during his reign; it was about establishing a legacy that would last long after he was gone. Augustus' careful cultivation of public favor created an enduring model of leadership that future Roman emperors would attempt to follow, ensuring that the strength of his rule was felt for generations to come. Soft power, in the hands of Augustus, became a powerful tool for not only maintaining control but for creating a lasting and beloved legacy.

Public Games and Bread: Augustus' Use of "Bread and Circuses" to Maintain Public Approval

AUGUSTUS UNDERSTOOD that keeping the Roman people content was crucial to maintaining his power. To achieve this, he employed the now-famous strategy of *panem et circenses*—"bread and circuses"—which involved providing the population with free food and extravagant entertainment. By focusing on the material needs and pleasures of the masses, Augustus secured their support and loyalty, ensuring that they were distracted from the concentration of political power in his hands.

The distribution of free grain was central to Augustus' approach. During the late Republic, Rome had developed a tradition of providing grain to its citizens, particularly the urban poor, to maintain stability. Augustus recognized the importance of this system and expanded it, regularizing the grain dole to make sure it was consistently available to a significant portion of the Roman population. His reforms to the grain supply, known as the *annona*, guaranteed that Rome had a steady flow of food from provinces like Egypt, which was annexed as a key supplier of grain.

These grain distributions served multiple purposes. They alleviated hunger among the poorer citizens, ensuring that the most vulnerable segments of society remained pacified. Moreover, they strengthened Augustus' image as a benevolent ruler who cared for the well-being of his people. By providing for their basic needs, Augustus fostered a sense of dependency and gratitude, reinforcing the idea that the emperor was the protector and provider of the Roman people. This social contract of sorts—the provision of food in exchange for public support—was a foundational element of Augustus' reign and helped stabilize his rule in the aftermath of years of civil war.

Entertainment was another vital component of Augustus' strategy to maintain public approval. Public games, or *ludi*, were already a beloved aspect of Roman life, and Augustus greatly expanded their scale and frequency. Gladiatorial contests, chariot races, theater performances, and mock naval battles were held regularly, offering the Roman people a welcome distraction from daily life and fostering a sense of shared civic pride. Augustus made sure that these spectacles were not only frequent but grand in scale, appealing to the Roman appetite for excitement and spectacle.

By personally sponsoring many of these games, Augustus positioned himself as the benefactor of public enjoyment. He used key moments, such as military victories, public anniversaries, or personal achievements, as occasions to hold large-scale games, ensuring that his personal achievements were always linked to the joy and entertainment of the people. These public events created a sense of unity and shared experience, solidifying his bond with the Roman populace.

To support these spectacles, Augustus invested heavily in public infrastructure, ensuring that Rome had the venues to host such large-scale events. He restored and expanded existing venues, such as the Circus Maximus, the largest chariot racing stadium in Rome, and oversaw the completion of the Theater of Marcellus, which provided space for dramatic performances. He also built the Forum of Augustus, a grand public space that symbolized his commitment to both the people and the legacy of Rome. These venues became symbols of Roman grandeur, and by association, they enhanced Augustus' image as the ruler who had brought stability, prosperity, and entertainment back to the city.

Through this combination of material provision and entertainment, Augustus ensured that the Roman people were content and distracted from the more profound political changes happening around them. The policy of *bread and circuses* helped to deflect attention away from the erosion of the Republican institutions and the centralization of power under Augustus' control. By meeting the immediate needs of the population and offering them regular entertainment, Augustus secured the loyalty and goodwill of the people, making it easier for him to reshape Roman governance without widespread resistance.

Augustus' mastery of this strategy was not just about keeping the people happy in the short term. It was about creating a long-lasting system of support that could endure throughout his reign. The regular grain distributions and public games became ingrained in Roman life, ensuring that future emperors would continue these practices to maintain their own public approval. Augustus understood that governance was about more than military might or political strategy; it was about keeping the people invested in their ruler's success, and his use of bread and circuses became one of the most enduring aspects of his legacy.

Pater Patriae (Father of the Nation): Augustus as Protector and Provider of Rome

AUGUSTUS UNDERSTOOD that to maintain his power and secure his legacy, he needed to position himself not just as a military leader but as the protector and provider for the Roman people. In 2 BCE, Augustus was granted the title *Pater Patriae*, or "Father of the Nation," a title that encapsulated the image he had carefully cultivated throughout his reign. This title symbolized his role as a paternal figure who cared for all aspects of Roman life—military, civic, and moral. Augustus blended his military successes with a deep commitment to the welfare of the Roman state, reinforcing the idea that his leadership was essential to the prosperity and stability of Rome.

Augustus' military achievements were the foundation of his authority, but he understood that military prowess alone would not be enough to maintain long-term stability. After his victory over Mark Antony and Cleopatra, Augustus secured Rome's borders and expanded the empire, bringing new territories under Roman control and ensuring the security of the state. These victories provided Augustus with the political capital necessary to consolidate his power, but he knew that to be more than a conqueror, he needed to establish himself as the guarantor of peace and order within the empire. By presenting himself as the defender of Roman security, Augustus justified his position at the top of the political hierarchy, while emphasizing that his rule was essential for maintaining Rome's military dominance.

Beyond his military success, Augustus took great care to present himself as the provider of civic stability and prosperity. He focused on public works and infrastructure projects that enhanced the quality of life in Rome, such as building new roads, aqueducts, and public buildings. By investing in these civic improvements, Augustus demonstrated that he was not only a ruler focused on external conquests but also a leader dedicated to the well-being of his people. His construction of the Forum of Augustus, the Temple of Mars Ultor, and the Ara Pacis were symbols of his commitment to the city's physical and spiritual renewal. These projects were more than monuments—they were expressions of Augustus' role as the protector of Roman traditions and the provider of civic pride and unity.

Augustus also took steps to improve the social fabric of Roman life, introducing legal and moral reforms that reinforced his image as a paternal figure. His moral legislation, such as the *lex Julia*, promoted marriage, family values, and public morality, reinforcing the idea that the stability of Rome depended on the virtue of its citizens. By linking the health of the Roman state to the behavior of its people, Augustus positioned himself as the moral guide of the empire, responsible for ensuring the continuity of Rome's greatness through the promotion of traditional values.

In his role as *Pater Patriae*, Augustus carefully balanced the image of a powerful military leader with that of a benevolent father figure, dedicated to the welfare of the people. **He sought to create a sense of personal loyalty and attachment among the Roman populace, presenting himself as the indispensable figure who had brought peace, prosperity, and stability to Rome after decades of civil war.** This paternal image was reinforced through his public speeches, monuments, and legal reforms, which consistently emphasized his role as the guardian of Roman values and protector of the state.

The title of *Pater Patriae* was the culmination of Augustus' decades-long effort to blend his military achievements with civic responsibility. It symbolized not only his political dominance but also his moral authority over Rome. By branding himself as the father of the Roman people, Augustus created an enduring image that went beyond that of a typical ruler—he became the embodiment of Roman stability, security, and prosperity. This image allowed him to command respect and loyalty from all segments of Roman society, from the Senate to the common people, and it ensured that his legacy would be seen not only as that of a great leader but also as the foundational figure of the Roman Empire.

Through the careful blending of military success and civic duty, Augustus created a model of leadership that positioned him as both a powerful ruler and a compassionate protector. **His role as *Pater Patriae* established a personal bond between Augustus and the Roman people, making him not only the leader of the state but also the symbolic father of the Roman nation.** This carefully crafted image played a critical role in the longevity of his rule, allowing Augustus to consolidate his authority while maintaining widespread public support. His legacy as *Pater Patriae* would resonate for centuries, shaping the role of future Roman emperors who sought to emulate his combination of strength, virtue, and paternal care for the empire.

Balancing Military Force with Popularity: Augustus' Strategy for Enduring Power

AUGUSTUS' RISE TO POWER was built on military victories, but his long-term success as Rome's first emperor came from his ability to balance the use of military force with a deep connection to the people. While his military achievements solidified his authority in the early years, Augustus understood that relying solely on the army to maintain control would not ensure the stability of his rule or the loyalty of the Roman populace. Instead, he built a broad base of support through public works, social policies, and a personal relationship with the people, positioning himself not just as a military leader, but as a ruler who cared deeply for the prosperity and well-being of Roman society.

After defeating Mark Antony and Cleopatra in 31 BCE, Augustus emerged as the uncontested leader of Rome, commanding vast military resources. His control over the legions and his ability to secure Rome's borders allowed him to end decades of civil war and bring relative peace to the empire. However, Augustus recognized that maintaining power solely through military dominance risked alienating the Senate and the Roman elite, as well as the general population. To avoid the perception of being a tyrant who ruled by force, Augustus cleverly transitioned from a military conqueror to a civic benefactor, using his victories to promote peace and stability within Rome itself.

Public works and infrastructure projects became a key tool in Augustus' strategy to connect with the people and secure his popularity. He invested heavily in the physical transformation of Rome, restoring and building temples, forums, roads, aqueducts, and public buildings that would improve the daily lives of Roman citizens. His ambitious construction projects, such as the Forum of Augustus, the Pantheon, and the Aqua Virgo aqueduct, symbolized the renewal of the city under his leadership. By beautifying Rome and enhancing its infrastructure, Augustus associated his rule with progress, stability, and the revitalization of the empire. These projects not only improved the quality of life but also created thousands of jobs, ensuring that the populace benefited directly from his reign.

Beyond physical infrastructure, Augustus implemented social policies that further strengthened his bond with the people. Recognizing the importance of food security in an increasingly urbanized Roman population, Augustus reformed the grain supply system, ensuring that the distribution of free or subsidized grain became more regular and reliable. This system, known as the *annona*, was vital for keeping the urban poor content, and by ensuring the steady flow of grain from provinces such as Egypt, Augustus presented himself as a ruler who cared for the basic needs of his people. This direct provision of essential resources helped to build a personal connection between Augustus and the Roman populace, who saw him as a protector and provider.

In addition to providing for the people's material needs, Augustus cultivated a sense of unity and civic pride through large-scale public spectacles. These games and festivals were carefully orchestrated to celebrate Augustus' achievements and Rome's newfound stability, while also giving the people regular opportunities for entertainment and leisure. Gladiatorial contests, chariot races, theater performances, and religious festivals were all expanded under Augustus' rule, ensuring that the Roman people felt both entertained and engaged in the life of the empire. By sponsoring these spectacles, Augustus positioned himself as the benefactor of public joy, further ingraining his popularity.

Augustus also used legal and moral reforms to strengthen his relationship with the Roman people, reinforcing traditional values and promoting social stability. Through laws such as the *lex Julia,*

Augustus encouraged marriage, family life, and the production of children, particularly among the upper classes. These laws were aimed at reversing social decline and reinforcing the importance of the family unit, which Augustus viewed as essential to the stability of Rome. His focus on morality also allowed him to present himself as a moral leader who was restoring the greatness of Rome by addressing not just its physical infrastructure, but its social and moral fabric.

At the same time, Augustus was careful not to diminish the importance of the military, recognizing that his power still depended on the loyalty of the legions. He restructured the Roman army, creating a professional, standing military that was more disciplined and loyal to the emperor. Augustus established the *aerarium militare*, a military treasury that provided for the payment and retirement of soldiers, ensuring their financial security and deepening their loyalty to him. By securing the army's well-being, Augustus maintained the support of the military without needing to rely solely on its force to govern.

Augustus' ability to balance military might with popularity was key to his enduring rule. He carefully cultivated his image as both a military victor and a civic leader who was deeply invested in the well-being of the Roman people. His public works, social policies, and moral reforms were all part of a broader strategy to build a personal connection with the populace, ensuring that they viewed him not as a distant or oppressive ruler but as a benefactor and protector. This combination of military strength and civic investment allowed Augustus to maintain control of Rome for over 40 years, creating a foundation of stability and peace that would last long after his death.

Ultimately, Augustus' legacy was not just about his military achievements but about how he used his power to transform Rome into a prosperous, stable, and unified empire. His reign demonstrated that long-term rule required more than the might of the sword—it required the ability to win the loyalty and support of the people through tangible improvements to their daily lives and a sense of shared purpose. By balancing military force with popularity, Augustus ensured that his reign would be remembered as one of the most successful and transformative in Roman history.

Chapter 7: Propaganda and Myth-Making — The Divine Augustus

Augustus understood early in his rise to power that controlling the narrative surrounding his leadership was essential for maintaining authority and securing his legacy. To achieve this, he masterfully blended propaganda and myth-making, intertwining his rule with the gods and the foundational myths of Rome. Augustus was more than a political leader—he became a symbol of divine favor, a figure whose power was preordained and whose reign was part of Rome's destiny.

Through the calculated use of religious symbolism, public monuments, literature, and art, Augustus crafted a narrative that positioned him as a ruler chosen by the gods to restore peace and stability to Rome after years of civil war. His divine lineage, connecting him to Venus through Julius Caesar, was central to this image. It allowed him to claim that his rise to power was not a product of ambition but a fulfillment of divine will. By carefully cultivating this godlike image, Augustus ensured that his authority was seen as not only legitimate but as an integral part of Rome's cosmic order.

In this chapter, the focus is on how Augustus used propaganda and myth-making to shape his image, solidifying his position as both a ruler and a semi-divine figure. His strategic use of these tools helped him secure the loyalty of the Roman people, legitimize his rule, and establish a legacy that would last for centuries. Through propaganda, Augustus didn't just rule Rome—he shaped how Rome would remember him, intertwining his personal story with the myths and legends that defined the Roman world.

Augustus' Deification: Using Divine Ancestry to Legitimize His Rule

AUGUSTUS SKILLFULLY used the idea of his divine ancestry to reinforce and legitimize his rule, weaving it into the fabric of Roman politics and society. After the assassination of Julius Caesar, Augustus, then known as Octavian, was quick to capitalize on Caesar's deification by the Senate in 42 BCE. As Caesar was officially declared a god, Augustus positioned himself as the *Divi Filius*—the "son of the divine," claiming a direct link to divinity. This status gave Augustus a powerful advantage in the Roman political landscape, where religion and politics were deeply intertwined.

Augustus traced his divine lineage back further, using his supposed connection to the goddess Venus. As Julius Caesar had claimed descent from Aeneas, the legendary Trojan hero and son of Venus, Augustus could reinforce his legitimacy by aligning himself with Rome's mythological foundations. By claiming descent from Venus, Augustus connected himself to both the divine and the very origins of Rome. This divine ancestry gave him an aura of exceptionalism and destiny, portraying his rise to power as preordained by the gods.

This divine status wasn't just a matter of personal belief; Augustus used it as a political tool to solidify his rule. By portraying himself as divinely favored, Augustus made it difficult for his political opponents to challenge him without appearing to defy the gods themselves. His divine lineage became an integral part of his public persona, appearing on coins, in literature, and in public ceremonies. The imagery of Augustus as a divinely ordained ruler was also propagated through monuments such as the Temple of Julius Caesar, built to honor his adoptive father and reinforce the divine connection between Augustus and the Roman state.

This idea of divine ancestry also played a central role in Augustus' self-deification later in his reign. While Augustus never explicitly claimed to be a god during his lifetime, he was careful to promote the idea that his rule was divinely sanctioned. This laid the groundwork for his eventual deification after his death in 14 CE, when the Senate officially declared him a god. The cult of the emperor became an important part of Roman religion, with temples and priests dedicated to Augustus and the emperors who followed him. By linking his rule to the divine, Augustus established a legacy that went beyond mortal politics, cementing his status as the founder of a new era for Rome.

Through this clever use of divine ancestry, Augustus was able to craft an image of himself as not just a political leader, but a figure whose authority was rooted in the divine order. This divine narrative served as a powerful tool to legitimize his rule and solidify his place as the supreme leader of Rome. His self-presentation as *Divi Filius* ensured that his reign was seen as not just necessary, but destined, adding a layer of sacred authority that transcended mere political power. In doing so, Augustus created a framework for future emperors to follow, blending political authority with divine right, ensuring that his legacy would endure both in this world and in the realm of the gods.

The Cult of Augustus: Encouraging a Personal Cult to Cement His Divine Image

AUGUSTUS CAREFULLY cultivated the development of a personal cult around himself, elevating his image beyond that of a mere political leader and into the realm of divinity. This process was gradual and strategic, reinforcing Augustus' authority as not only the ruler of Rome but also as a figure worthy of worship. By the end of his reign, the cult of Augustus was firmly established, with temples, statues, and rituals dedicated to honoring him as a semi-divine figure, linking his political authority with religious reverence.

One of Augustus' key strategies was allowing the formation of his cult outside of Rome first, particularly in the provinces. In many of the eastern provinces, where ruler cults were already common, Augustus encouraged the people to worship him as a living deity. This allowed Augustus to test the waters of his own deification without directly challenging traditional Roman values, which were initially more resistant to the idea of a living god. In cities such as Ephesus and Pergamum, temples were built in his honor, and he was worshiped alongside Roman gods. This blending of traditional Roman religion with emperor worship helped to reinforce Augustus' image as divinely favored and set the stage for his eventual deification after his death.

In Rome itself, Augustus was more cautious, but he still laid the groundwork for his cult. While he did not openly declare himself a god during his lifetime, he fostered a religious aura around his rule. He associated himself with gods like Apollo and Mars, aligning his leadership with the divine protection and favor of Rome. Augustus also encouraged the veneration of his family, particularly Julius Caesar, whose deification by the Senate Augustus used to his advantage by claiming the title *Divi Filius* ("Son of the Divine"). This familial connection to divinity was a critical part of the cult of Augustus, emphasizing the idea that his rule was sanctioned by the gods.

The construction of the Ara Pacis and other monuments played a significant role in promoting Augustus' divine status. The Ara Pacis, or Altar of Peace, was a symbol of the peace and prosperity that Augustus had brought to the empire, a testament to his godlike ability to restore order to a fractured Rome. Statues and temples were dedicated to him across the empire, further solidifying his position as a ruler whose authority transcended the political and entered the sacred.

Augustus' subtle encouragement of his cult during his lifetime laid the foundation for his deification after his death in 14 CE. Upon his death, the Senate officially declared him a god, and the worship of Augustus became an integral part of Roman state religion. Temples were built in his honor, and the practice of emperor worship, which had begun with Augustus, became a central element of Roman religious life for centuries. Augustus' careful cultivation of his image ensured that his rule would not only be remembered politically but also revered religiously.

By fostering the formation of a personal cult, Augustus ensured that his legacy extended beyond the mortal realm. He was not just a ruler but a figure who commanded spiritual reverence, a man whose authority was intertwined with the divine. This blending of political leadership and religious worship allowed Augustus to solidify his power during his lifetime and ensure his lasting influence after death. The cult of Augustus created a template for future emperors, making the divine authority of the ruler a cornerstone of the Roman Empire's ideological foundation.

Symbolism in Rhetoric and Art: Augustus' Use of Religious Symbolism to Reinforce His Godlike Status

AUGUSTUS WAS A MASTER of using symbolism in both rhetoric and art to elevate his image and reinforce his godlike status. Throughout his reign, he carefully crafted his public image by integrating religious and divine motifs into various mediums, from statues and coins to public monuments. This visual and rhetorical symbolism was not only meant to celebrate his accomplishments but also to subtly suggest that his rule was sanctioned by the gods, solidifying his position as a semi-divine figure in the eyes of the Roman people.

In statues, Augustus employed religious symbolism to present himself as a figure who transcended mortal leadership. One of the most iconic representations of this is the statue of Augustus of Prima Porta. In this statue, Augustus is depicted in military garb, but the imagery goes far beyond that of a typical Roman general. His breastplate is adorned with mythological and divine figures, including Apollo and Diana, reinforcing his connection to the gods. Furthermore, a small figure of Cupid is depicted riding a dolphin at Augustus' feet, symbolizing his divine descent from Venus through Aeneas, the legendary founder of Rome. This imagery was intended to communicate Augustus' divinely ordained rule, making it clear that his authority came not just from military victories but from the gods themselves.

Coins were another medium through which Augustus spread his divine symbolism. As the currency of the Roman Empire, coins were a powerful way to disseminate imagery that reinforced Augustus' godlike status. Coins minted during his reign often bore his portrait, but more importantly, they featured symbols and deities associated with his rule. Apollo and Mars, gods linked to peace and war, frequently appeared alongside Augustus, suggesting that his leadership balanced both divine protection and military might. On other coins, symbols like the laurel wreath, associated with victory and immortality, were used to underscore Augustus' role as the eternal protector of Rome. By associating himself with such divine symbols, Augustus positioned himself as more than a mortal ruler—he was part of a cosmic order that ensured Rome's greatness.

Public monuments and altars also carried profound religious symbolism, linking Augustus directly to the gods. The Ara Pacis, or Altar of Peace, is one of the most famous examples of how Augustus used religious symbolism in public art to reinforce his godlike image. This monument, commissioned to celebrate the peace brought by Augustus' reign, features a wealth of religious and mythological imagery. The friezes depict figures from Roman mythology, fertility symbols, and the gods themselves, all woven together to suggest that Augustus' rule was in harmony with the divine will. The imagery conveys the idea that Augustus had restored cosmic and earthly order, further embedding the notion that his leadership was blessed by the gods.

Religious symbolism was also woven into Augustus' rhetoric, strengthening the association between his rule and the divine. In his public speeches and written works, Augustus often referenced his divine ancestry and the favor of the gods. By emphasizing his descent from Venus through Julius Caesar, whom the Senate had declared a god, Augustus crafted a narrative that his rule was destined and preordained. In official proclamations, he frequently invoked the gods to validate his decisions, suggesting that his actions were aligned with divine plans for Rome. This fusion of religious and political rhetoric created an unbreakable link between Augustus' authority and the will of the gods.

The use of religious symbolism was a deliberate and strategic way for Augustus to elevate his status and cement his legacy. By integrating divine imagery into his public persona through statues, coins, monuments, and rhetoric, Augustus made his rule seem inevitable and unassailable. The symbolism not only glorified his achievements but also made opposition to him appear as opposition to the gods themselves. This blend of political power with religious imagery became a crucial part of Augustus' lasting legacy and set the standard for future emperors, who would continue to use art and rhetoric to project their own divine status.

In the end, Augustus' use of religious symbolism was more than mere propaganda—it was a calculated strategy to intertwine his rule with the gods, ensuring that his authority was perceived as divinely ordained. By presenting himself as a ruler favored by the divine, Augustus was able to transcend the limitations of mortal leadership and secure a godlike status that would endure long after his death. Through this clever use of art and rhetoric, Augustus not only controlled the political narrative of his reign but also shaped how he would be remembered for centuries to come.

Key Takeaway: The Enduring Power of Myth-Making in Consolidating Long-Term Influence and Legacy

AUGUSTUS' REIGN PROVIDES a striking example of how myth-making can serve as a potent tool for consolidating power, securing influence, and shaping a lasting legacy. His mastery of blending political achievements with divine imagery allowed him to craft a narrative that framed his rule as both inevitable and divinely sanctioned. This strategy not only elevated him above his rivals but also ingrained his leadership into the fabric of Roman culture, ensuring that his legacy would endure long after his death.

One of the central components of Augustus' myth-making was his emphasis on divine ancestry. By claiming descent from Venus through his adoptive father, Julius Caesar, who had been deified by the Senate, Augustus linked his authority to the gods themselves. This divine connection was reinforced through public art, statues, and coinage, which depicted him alongside figures like Venus, Apollo, and Mars. By constantly presenting himself as favored by the gods, Augustus created a perception that opposing him was not merely a political act, but a challenge to the cosmic order. This elevated status helped cement his position as Rome's leader, making him appear irreplaceable and unassailable.

Augustus also utilized public monuments to solidify this mythological image. Structures like the Ara Pacis (Altar of Peace) and the Forum of Augustus were designed not only to celebrate his achievements but also to project a sense of divine endorsement. The imagery in these monuments, from scenes of fertility and prosperity to representations of mythological figures, linked Augustus' reign to the blessings of the gods. This myth-making through architecture ensured that the physical landscape of Rome itself became a testament to his rule, reinforcing his authority every time a citizen passed by these symbols of divine favor.

In addition to physical symbols, Augustus' rhetoric was carefully designed to align his leadership with Rome's foundational myths. He positioned himself as the restorer of the Republic, a figure who had brought peace after decades of civil war, all while gradually consolidating his power. By casting himself as the protector of Roman traditions and values, Augustus made it appear that his leadership was not a departure from the Republic but a continuation of its highest ideals. His speeches and written works frequently invoked the gods and Rome's legendary past, blending the historical with the mythological to make his rule seem like a natural and necessary extension of Rome's destiny.

The personal cult Augustus encouraged further expanded the myth surrounding his life and reign. Though cautious not to overtly claim divinity during his lifetime in Rome, Augustus allowed worship of his person to spread in the provinces, where ruler cults were already common. This laid the groundwork for his official deification after his death, when the Senate declared him a god. By fostering this divine narrative during his life and securing his place among the gods after death, Augustus ensured that his influence would transcend the mortal realm. His deification provided a powerful example for future emperors, creating a precedent where the line between ruler and god became increasingly blurred.

The myth-making employed by Augustus was not just about securing immediate political control; it was about shaping how he would be remembered for centuries to come. By embedding his rule within Rome's religious, cultural, and historical traditions, Augustus ensured that his image would be immortalized in the hearts and minds of Romans. His ability to present himself as both a mortal ruler and a divine figure allowed him to craft a legacy that was as much about symbolism and perception as it was about politics and military success.

Augustus' success in using myth-making to consolidate power demonstrates the enduring importance of controlling one's own narrative. By shaping how he was perceived, both during his life and after his death, Augustus was able to create a legacy that not only justified his power but also immortalized him as the founder of a new era for Rome. This lasting influence is a testament to the power of myth—the ability to turn historical actions into legends, and to use those legends to maintain influence long after the events themselves have passed.

The lessons from Augustus' use of myth-making extend far beyond his time. Leaders throughout history have understood that crafting a compelling narrative—whether through religious symbolism, art, or cultural tradition—can elevate their authority and secure their place in history. Augustus' reign shows that building and controlling myths is not merely about embellishing the past but about shaping the future. His blend of political savvy, religious symbolism, and cultural integration allowed him to build an empire that would be remembered for centuries, and his example continues to resonate as a case study in how myth can be used to sustain influence and create an enduring legacy.

Chapter 8: The Succession Plan — Ensuring the Empire's Future

Augustus understood that his personal rule was only the beginning of Rome's transformation from a republic to an empire. His long-term vision for Rome required more than just consolidating power during his lifetime—it required ensuring that his successors could maintain the stability and prosperity he had brought to the empire. Succession was one of the most challenging and delicate issues he faced, especially in a system where the traditional mechanisms for transferring power had been eroded. The future of the empire depended on a smooth, carefully managed transition of power, which Augustus approached with characteristic foresight and caution.

In shaping the future of Rome, Augustus knew he had to craft a robust and durable succession plan, involving not only his immediate family but also trusted allies who could carry forward his policies and maintain the unity of the empire. His experience with the deaths of key heirs like Gaius and Lucius Caesar forced him to continually adjust his strategy, but his goal remained the same: securing the empire's future through a stable, legitimate line of succession. By balancing family dynamics, political alliances, and the demands of the Roman people, Augustus carefully curated his successors to ensure that his legacy—and the empire—would endure long after his death.

This chapter explores how Augustus approached the vital task of planning for succession, examining the steps he took to groom potential heirs, manage political expectations, and create a seamless transition of power. Through his meticulous strategy, Augustus set the foundation for the continuation of his dynasty and ensured the long-term stability of the Roman Empire.

The Tiberius Dilemma: Ensuring a Stable Transition of Power

AS AUGUSTUS AGED, ONE of his greatest challenges was securing a stable transition of power. His careful management of succession was crucial to maintaining the long-term stability of the Roman Empire he had built. Augustus' chosen heir, Tiberius, was not the most obvious or popular choice, and the process of grooming him for leadership was a delicate balancing act. Augustus needed to ensure that Tiberius' ascent would not be contested, while simultaneously managing other potential rivals, such as Marcus Agrippa and Germanicus, who had strong claims to power or popular support.

Augustus' first attempt at managing succession was through his marriage to Livia Drusilla, and the promotion of her sons, Tiberius and Drusus, as potential heirs. However, Augustus initially seemed to favor Marcus Agrippa, his close friend and military commander, as his successor. Agrippa had been instrumental in many of Augustus' victories, including the decisive Battle of Actium, and was a trusted advisor and administrator. Augustus solidified Agrippa's position by marrying him to his daughter, Julia, effectively making Agrippa part of the imperial family. This move ensured that Agrippa was not only a loyal subordinate but also a potential candidate for the continuation of Augustus' dynasty.

However, Agrippa's death in 12 BCE forced Augustus to reconsider his plans for succession. With Agrippa gone, Augustus turned his attention to the younger generation, particularly his grandsons Gaius and Lucius Caesar, who were the sons of Julia and Agrippa. Augustus adopted both boys and began grooming them as his future heirs, positioning them as the future leaders of Rome. Statues, coins, and other public symbols highlighted their importance, signaling to the Roman people that they would eventually take on

Augustus' mantle. Yet tragedy struck again when both Gaius and Lucius died prematurely, leaving Augustus with no obvious successor from the younger generation.

This succession crisis left Augustus with a difficult decision: whether to elevate Tiberius, his stepson, as his heir. Tiberius was a capable military leader, but he lacked the charm and popularity of other potential successors like Agrippa and Germanicus, Augustus' great-nephew. Augustus had often overlooked Tiberius in favor of other candidates, but with Gaius and Lucius gone, Tiberius became the most viable option. To ensure a smooth transition, Augustus adopted Tiberius formally in 4 CE, making him his legal son and heir. However, this was not enough on its own; Augustus needed to solidify Tiberius' legitimacy and ensure that no other rivals could challenge his position.

One of Augustus' most significant concerns was managing the popularity of Germanicus, who was both a member of the Julio-Claudian dynasty and a rising star in the Roman military. Germanicus, the son of Drusus (Tiberius' brother) and a great-nephew of Augustus, was widely loved by the Roman people and the legions due to his military successes. Augustus had to walk a fine line between promoting Germanicus' talents and ensuring that his popularity did not overshadow Tiberius. To mitigate any potential rivalry, Augustus arranged for Tiberius to adopt Germanicus as his son, effectively making Germanicus the designated successor after Tiberius. This move helped to balance the power dynamics within the family and ensured that Germanicus remained loyal to Tiberius, rather than positioning himself as an alternative leader.

Augustus was also careful to control the military careers of his potential heirs, knowing that military success could easily translate into political ambition. While Tiberius and Germanicus were both given important commands, Augustus kept a tight rein on their activities, ensuring that they remained loyal to him and did not cultivate independent power bases within the army. By maintaining control over their military appointments and public appearances, Augustus minimized the risk that either figure could use their popularity or military strength to challenge his authority or the planned succession.

In addition to managing potential rivals, Augustus took great care to prepare Tiberius for leadership through a gradual transfer of responsibilities. Over the years, Augustus increasingly involved Tiberius in the administration of the empire, allowing him to take on key military and political roles. By the time of Augustus' death in 14 CE, Tiberius had already acted as co-ruler in all but name, ensuring a smooth transition of power. Augustus' strategy of slowly integrating Tiberius into the governance of the empire gave the Roman people time to accept him as their future leader, reducing the likelihood of unrest after Augustus' death.

The ultimate success of Augustus' succession plan was seen in the relatively smooth transition of power to Tiberius, despite the challenges posed by popular figures like Germanicus. Through careful management of potential rivals and a deliberate transfer of authority, Augustus was able to secure the continuity of his regime and establish a precedent for future successions within the Roman Empire. By ensuring that Tiberius had both the legal standing and the experience needed to govern, Augustus safeguarded the stability of Rome and the legacy of his reign.

The Tiberius dilemma highlights Augustus' skillful approach to succession planning, balancing family dynamics, political alliances, and public perception to ensure a stable transition of power. Rather than relying on force or favoritism, Augustus employed a calculated and pragmatic strategy that took into account the ambitions and popularity of those around him, ensuring that his chosen heir would face minimal opposition. This careful orchestration of succession set the standard for how future emperors would manage the delicate process of transferring power in an empire that was built as much on perception and loyalty as on military might.

Shaping the Future of Rome: Augustus' Careful Curation of Family and Allies for Leadership Roles

AUGUSTUS UNDERSTOOD that securing the future stability of Rome required careful planning and the strategic placement of his family and trusted allies into key leadership roles. He knew that the empire he had built could only endure if those in power after him were loyal to his vision and capable of maintaining the delicate balance of authority and governance he had established. Over the years, Augustus meticulously curated a network of family members and close allies, grooming them to take up critical roles within the Roman state and ensuring that his legacy would continue long after his death.

One of Augustus' primary strategies for shaping the future leadership of Rome was through his family. He carefully arranged marriages and adoptions to strengthen familial ties and ensure that his bloodline remained at the center of Roman politics. Marriages within his family were not simply personal matters but strategic alliances designed to consolidate power. His daughter Julia, for example, was married to key figures such as Marcus Agrippa and, later, Tiberius, both of whom played crucial roles in Augustus' plans for succession. These marriages bound his potential successors closer to the Julian-Claudian dynasty, ensuring their loyalty to Augustus' vision for Rome.

Augustus also used the tool of adoption to control succession and ensure continuity. Roman tradition allowed for the adoption of heirs, and Augustus leveraged this practice to secure the future of his dynasty. He famously adopted his grandsons Gaius and Lucius Caesar, the sons of Julia and Agrippa, positioning them as his chosen heirs and grooming them for leadership from a young age. Although their premature deaths forced Augustus to reconsider his succession plans, these adoptions demonstrated his foresight in shaping the future leadership of Rome through familial ties.

As Augustus' attention turned to Tiberius, his stepson through his marriage to Livia Drusilla, he ensured that Tiberius was fully integrated into the structures of Roman power. Augustus adopted Tiberius formally in 4 CE, solidifying his legal claim to succession. Over time, Augustus increasingly delegated military and administrative duties to Tiberius, allowing him to build a reputation as a capable leader. This gradual transfer of authority helped to ensure that Tiberius would be accepted as the legitimate ruler after Augustus' death, despite some reservations within the Roman elite.

Close allies outside the family were also pivotal in Augustus' plans for the future of Rome. Marcus Agrippa, one of Augustus' most trusted generals and advisors, was essential to Augustus' early successes and was positioned as a potential successor before his untimely death. Agrippa's marriage to Julia tied him directly to the Julian dynasty, and he played a critical role in shaping the empire's infrastructure and military capabilities. Even after Agrippa's death, Augustus ensured that his legacy lived on through his children, Gaius and Lucius, who were intended to carry on the Julian name.

Germanicus, another key figure in Augustus' network, was similarly managed to maintain stability and loyalty within the empire. Germanicus was an enormously popular general and the son of Augustus' nephew, Drusus. Recognizing Germanicus' popularity with both the Roman people and the legions, Augustus arranged for him to be adopted by Tiberius, thus binding the two most important figures of the Julio-Claudian dynasty. This move not only quelled any potential rivalry between Germanicus and Tiberius but also ensured that the next generation of leadership remained within Augustus' carefully curated family circle.

Augustus also placed his allies in key political positions to secure their influence after his death. He rewarded loyalty and competence with high-ranking positions in the Roman Senate, the military, and the provincial governments. By surrounding himself with capable and loyal individuals, Augustus ensured that the empire's governance would remain in trusted hands, even after his passing. These allies helped maintain the stability of Rome during his reign, and Augustus' careful placement of them in positions of power created a solid foundation for the continuation of his policies and vision.

The way Augustus curated his family and allies to hold leadership roles after his death was a testament to his foresight and understanding of Roman politics. He recognized that Rome's future depended not just on a single successor but on a network of individuals who were loyal to the empire's stability and continuity. By promoting a combination of family members and trusted allies, Augustus created a system of governance that was more resilient than any single ruler. His legacy was built not only on his own achievements but also on the lasting structures and relationships he cultivated among those who would follow him.

Through these carefully crafted familial connections, adoptions, and political alliances, Augustus shaped the future of Rome in a way that would allow the empire to thrive long after his death. His ability to manage succession, control the placement of key allies, and ensure loyalty within his inner circle ensured that his legacy would endure, even as new leaders took his place. Augustus' meticulous planning for the future was critical in maintaining the stability of the Roman Empire and securing his place as one of the most successful rulers in history.

Key Takeaway: The Importance of Planning for Succession to Ensure the Continued Survival of a Regime

AUGUSTUS' REIGN PROVIDES a masterclass in the importance of succession planning for the stability and longevity of a regime. Recognizing that his personal achievements would not be enough to guarantee the survival of Rome's newfound stability, Augustus focused on grooming successors and strategically placing family members and allies in positions of power. His calculated approach to ensuring a smooth transition of authority allowed him to protect the empire he had built and ensure that his policies and vision would endure.

Augustus didn't leave succession to chance; he carefully selected and prepared his heirs, managing both the internal dynamics of his family and the political realities of Rome. Through adoption, marriage, and the delegation of authority, he created a web of relationships that tied his chosen successors to the Julio-Claudian dynasty. This foresight prevented power struggles that might have destabilized the empire, ensuring a continuity of leadership that maintained the strength and unity of the regime after his death.

Moreover, Augustus understood that succession planning was about more than just choosing a single heir. By placing trusted allies and loyalists in key positions within the Senate, military, and provincial governments, Augustus built a network of supporters who would uphold the empire's structure even after his passing. This network of familial and political connections made it more difficult for any one individual to disrupt the stability of the empire, safeguarding the regime from internal conflict or rival factions.

The careful planning of succession is a vital lesson from Augustus' reign. By ensuring that power passed smoothly to capable and loyal successors, Augustus protected his legacy and the future of the Roman Empire. His strategy highlights the necessity for long-term thinking in leadership, emphasizing that the survival of a regime depends on the structures and people left in place after a ruler's departure. Augustus' legacy endures not only because of his personal achievements but because of the careful, deliberate steps he took to secure the empire's future.

Chapter 9: The Emperor's Balancing Act — Navigating Military and Civilian Roles

Augustus' reign marked a pivotal transformation in Roman governance, transitioning from the chaos of the late Republic to the structure of the Roman Empire. As the first emperor, Augustus was acutely aware that maintaining control over Rome required more than the brute force that had characterized the rise of many leaders before him. The balance between wielding military power and managing civilian governance became the cornerstone of his leadership strategy, ensuring that he maintained authority without appearing as a tyrant. This delicate balancing act was critical in an era where the memory of Julius Caesar's assassination still loomed large—demonstrating how quickly perceived autocracy could lead to downfall.

To secure Rome's stability, Augustus had to strike a balance between his role as commander-in-chief of the legions and as a protector of the Republic's values. The Roman people and Senate were deeply attached to the ideals of the Republic, even as the reality of Augustus' reign centralized power in his hands. To navigate this, Augustus was careful to portray his military role as one of defense and peacekeeping rather than conquest for personal glory. Simultaneously, he worked to maintain the outward appearance of Republican governance by restoring and respecting institutions like the Senate, even though real power resided with him.

Furthermore, Augustus understood the potential threat posed by ambitious military commanders. He kept the legions loyal through financial incentives like the *aerarium militare* and kept control of provinces with the most military strength, avoiding the mistakes of past leaders who allowed generals to amass personal armies. However, he also ensured that his military achievements were carefully integrated into his civil role as the *Princeps*, making him not just the protector of the empire, but its stabilizing force. This dual identity as a leader rooted in military achievement and civic responsibility allowed Augustus to foster loyalty both from the army and from the Roman people.

This chapter will delve into the strategies Augustus employed to maintain this balance, exploring how he cultivated an image of strength without succumbing to the trappings of a military despot, while simultaneously governing a complex and vast empire. His ability to navigate these competing roles of military commander and civil ruler was essential not only to his personal success but to the longevity of the Roman Empire itself, shaping the framework for imperial leadership for centuries to come.

Balancing Autocracy and Republicanism: Augustus' Mastery in Presenting Himself as a Servant of the Republic

AUGUSTUS WAS A MASTER at walking the fine line between autocracy and the outward appearance of Republican values. Throughout his reign, he wielded near-absolute power, yet managed to maintain the façade that the Roman Republic was still functioning under its traditional institutions. This delicate balance was key to his long-term success, as it allowed him to consolidate power without provoking the kind of backlash that had led to Julius Caesar's assassination. By presenting himself as the *Princeps* (first citizen) and a humble servant of the Republic, Augustus created an image of himself as a leader who ruled in the best interest of the state, rather than as a monarch or tyrant.

Augustus' approach to power began with the *First Settlement* of 27 BCE, when he publicly "restored" the Republic to the Senate and the Roman people. In this carefully orchestrated event, Augustus offered to relinquish his extraordinary powers, but the Senate, in gratitude, awarded him new titles and control over the key provinces where the majority of Rome's legions were stationed. This clever maneuver allowed Augustus to retain control of the military—arguably the most important tool for maintaining power—while appearing to act with humility and respect for the Republic's institutions. By positioning himself as the protector of the Republic, rather than its conqueror, Augustus avoided the perception of despotism and retained the loyalty of the Roman elite.

At the heart of Augustus' strategy was his careful management of the Senate. While he stripped the Senate of much of its real power, he allowed it to continue functioning as a governing body, maintaining its role in Roman political life. Senators still met, debated, and passed laws, but Augustus controlled the most critical aspects of governance—especially military and foreign affairs—through his title of *Imperator* and his proconsular authority over Rome's key provinces. Augustus' ability to manipulate the Senate ensured that he could maintain the appearance of shared governance, while in practice he held the ultimate decision-making power. This arrangement satisfied the Roman aristocracy, who could still claim to have influence in state affairs, while Augustus remained the undisputed leader.

Another key aspect of Augustus' balancing act between autocracy and Republicanism was his use of traditional titles and roles. Rather than adopting the title of king or emperor, Augustus presented himself as the *Princeps*, or first citizen, a title that evoked the idea of service to the state. This was in stark contrast to the title of dictator, which had caused such resentment toward Julius Caesar. By taking on the role of *Princeps*, Augustus was able to portray his rule as a continuation of Republican traditions, even as he centralized authority in his own hands. His other titles, such as *Pontifex Maximus* (chief priest), further reinforced his image as a protector of Roman religion and values, linking his leadership to the preservation of Rome's cultural and spiritual heritage.

Augustus also maintained the illusion of Republican governance through the offices of consul and tribune. Although he held the consulship multiple times and later acquired the tribunician power for life, Augustus ensured that other members of the Roman elite continued to occupy these positions as well. This gave the impression that the old Republican offices were still relevant, even though Augustus' authority superseded them in practice. His lifelong tribunician power allowed him to introduce and veto legislation, ensuring that no laws could pass without his approval, while his repeated consulships placed him at the heart of Roman politics without appearing to outright dismantle the traditional system.

Public perception was a crucial component of Augustus' strategy. He carefully cultivated his image as a leader who acted in the best interests of the Roman people, rather than as a self-serving autocrat. Through monumental architecture, public works, and grain distributions, Augustus presented himself as a benefactor of the Roman populace. His patronage of the arts and literature, including works like Virgil's *Aeneid*, helped to create a narrative that tied Augustus' leadership to the divine will of the gods and the founding myths of Rome. By linking his rule to the restoration of peace, order, and prosperity after the chaos of the civil wars, Augustus legitimized his power and made it appear as though he was fulfilling a necessary role as the guardian of the Republic.

Augustus' careful balancing of autocratic control with Republican imagery was essential to the long-term stability of his regime. By maintaining the appearance of Republican governance, he avoided the perception of tyranny and prevented the kind of opposition that had brought down earlier leaders like Julius Caesar. This balance allowed Augustus to consolidate power without disrupting the traditions that the Roman elite and populace held dear, securing both their loyalty and the survival of his regime.

In the end, Augustus succeeded in crafting a new political system that allowed him to wield autocratic power while preserving the outward forms of the Republic. This system, known as the Principate, would endure for centuries, shaping the way future emperors ruled. By presenting himself as a servant of the state while maintaining control over the key instruments of power, Augustus was able to achieve the delicate balance between autocracy and Republicanism that allowed him to remain in power for over four decades and secure his place as one of Rome's most successful rulers.

Military Achievements and Governance: Balancing Military Leadership with Civil Rule

AUGUSTUS SKILLFULLY balanced his role as a military leader with his duties as a civil ruler, ensuring the Roman Empire remained stable while avoiding the dangers of military usurpation. His reign, built on the back of military victories, required careful management of the army to maintain control over Rome's territories without allowing any ambitious general to challenge his authority. Augustus' dual focus on governance and military success was essential to the longevity of his rule and the stability of the empire.

Augustus' military achievements were foundational to his consolidation of power. His victories in the civil wars, particularly the defeat of Mark Antony and Cleopatra at the Battle of Actium in 31 BCE, secured his control over the Roman world. These successes established him as Rome's premier military leader, giving him immense influence over the legions. However, Augustus knew that military power alone could not ensure the long-term stability of his reign. He had to transition from a wartime commander to a peacetime ruler, all while keeping the loyalty of the military and preventing any threats from rising within the ranks.

One of Augustus' first moves to maintain control over the military was his careful allocation of military command. After assuming power, he took control of Rome's most important provinces—those where the majority of the legions were stationed. These included strategically crucial areas like Gaul, Hispania, and Egypt. By placing these provinces under his direct command, Augustus ensured that he, rather than the Senate or other political leaders, had control over the most powerful military forces in the empire. This control over the legions was key to preventing any potential rivals from gaining enough support to challenge his authority.

Augustus also worked to professionalize and stabilize the Roman army, creating a standing military force that was loyal to the emperor rather than to individual generals. He reduced the number of legions from the bloated ranks of the civil war era, establishing a smaller, more manageable army that could be better controlled. To further ensure the loyalty of his soldiers, Augustus introduced the *aerarium militare*, a special military treasury set up to provide for the payment and retirement of soldiers. By guaranteeing financial security for the legions, Augustus secured their allegiance, making it clear that their well-being was directly tied to his leadership.

At the same time, Augustus was careful to avoid over-reliance on the military, presenting himself as a civil ruler who was dedicated to the peace and prosperity of Rome. His title of *Princeps*, or first citizen, emphasized his role as a civic leader rather than a military dictator. Augustus was keen to distance himself from the image of a ruler who depended solely on force, focusing instead on the restoration of Roman traditions and institutions. This balance between military power and civil authority helped to legitimize his rule and reassure the Roman Senate and people that Augustus was not a tyrant in the mold of Julius Caesar or earlier military strongmen.

Augustus also ensured that no single military commander could become too powerful or independent. By regularly rotating generals and avoiding long-term assignments in command positions, he prevented any one figure from developing a personal loyalty base among the legions. His treatment of key figures like Agrippa and Tiberius exemplified this strategy. Although Agrippa was one of Augustus' closest allies and most successful military commanders, Augustus ensured that Agrippa remained loyal by giving him key civil responsibilities and marrying him into the imperial family, binding him to the dynasty. Similarly, Tiberius, Augustus' eventual successor, was given command over the military but never allowed to wield unchecked power. Augustus always retained ultimate control, ensuring that the military was an extension of his authority rather than a source of independent power.

In addition to maintaining control over the military, Augustus used his civil rule to further reinforce his legitimacy. Through public works, legal reforms, and the promotion of moral legislation, Augustus presented himself as a ruler who was focused on the well-being of Rome and its people. He built roads, temples, and monuments, revitalized the Roman legal system, and implemented laws that encouraged marriage and family life. These actions reinforced the idea that Augustus was not just a military conqueror but a civil leader dedicated to restoring the glory of Rome. His public image was carefully crafted to balance his role as a protector of Rome with that of a benefactor who brought peace and stability.

Augustus' careful management of both the military and his civil responsibilities helped to create a stable and lasting system of governance. By balancing his authority as a military leader with his role as a civic ruler, Augustus prevented any potential usurpation from within the ranks of the army while maintaining the loyalty of the Roman people. His ability to shift from military victories to governance without relying solely on force allowed him to solidify his power and create the foundation for the Pax Romana, a period of relative peace and prosperity that would last for over two centuries.

In the end, Augustus' success lay in his ability to balance the dual aspects of his rule—military strength and civil leadership. He understood that long-term stability required more than just military victories; it demanded a delicate combination of force and governance, ensuring that Rome remained secure while also fostering a sense of unity and order within the empire. Through his strategic control of the military and his focus on civil rule, Augustus set a precedent for future emperors, establishing a model of leadership that would define Roman governance for generations to come.

Key Takeaway: The Delicate Balance Between Military Strength and Civilian Leadership is Crucial for Maintaining a Stable and Effective Rule

AUGUSTUS' REIGN ILLUSTRATES the importance of balancing military power with civilian leadership to ensure long-term stability. While his military achievements secured his initial rise to power, Augustus recognized that ruling solely through military force would lead to instability and potential challenges to his authority. Instead, he cultivated a role as both a military leader and a civil ruler, carefully managing the military while simultaneously restoring the traditions and institutions of Rome.

Augustus controlled the military by keeping direct command over the key provinces where the legions were stationed and professionalizing the army. By securing the loyalty of the soldiers through financial benefits and limiting the power of individual generals, he ensured that the military remained loyal to him, rather than allowing any one figure to become a threat to his leadership. This cautious approach prevented any single commander from gaining enough influence to challenge the emperor's authority.

At the same time, Augustus prioritized his role as a civil ruler, focusing on governance, public works, and legal reforms to present himself as a leader who cared for the Roman people. By portraying himself as the *Princeps*—a first among equals rather than a tyrant—Augustus created an image of humility and service, which was crucial in maintaining the support of both the Senate and the broader Roman populace. This balance between military might and civilian governance not only legitimized Augustus' rule but also established the foundation for the long-term stability of the Roman Empire.

The key lesson from Augustus' reign is that successful leadership requires a careful balance of military strength and civilian governance. Relying too heavily on the military can create instability and invite challenges from within, while focusing exclusively on civil leadership without military backing can leave a regime vulnerable to external threats. Augustus' ability to maintain this delicate balance ensured his effective rule and set the stage for one of the most prosperous periods in Roman history.

Chapter 10: Lessons for Modern Leaders — Applying Augustus' Strategy Today

Augustus' rise to power and his ability to maintain control over a vast empire for decades is a case study in effective leadership, demonstrating how foresight, strategy, and adaptability can lead to long-term success. Unlike many rulers who came before him, Augustus didn't rely solely on brute force or charisma; he carefully crafted a system of governance that ensured stability and security while balancing the expectations of various stakeholders—military, political elites, and the general populace. These are challenges that modern leaders across different sectors continue to face today.

Augustus understood that leadership is not just about achieving power but sustaining it over time. His reign was characterized by thoughtful decisions that ensured continuity, even after his death, through careful succession planning, the management of public perception, and the building of alliances that benefited not only him but also the people around him. This ability to create lasting institutions, delegate authority effectively, and secure long-term loyalty is something leaders today must prioritize if they aim to build enduring legacies.

In an era of rapid change and disruption, modern leaders—whether in politics, business, or social movements—must balance internal and external pressures much as Augustus did. Leaders today need to manage public perception in a world dominated by social media and instant communication, build strategic alliances in increasingly competitive markets, and navigate legal and regulatory frameworks that shape their industries. Augustus' ability to master these same dynamics in his time offers invaluable lessons for how today's leaders can similarly secure their positions and guide their organizations or nations to success.

This chapter will explore how the principles Augustus used to lead Rome into its golden age can be directly applied to modern leadership challenges, helping leaders navigate complexity, inspire loyalty, and build lasting influence in a world that, like Augustus', demands a careful balancing of power and perception. By examining how Augustus maintained his grip on power and legitimacy, leaders today can draw practical lessons on how to govern effectively in an interconnected and ever-changing landscape.

Practical Lessons from Augustus: Applying His Strategies to Modern Leadership and Power Structures

AUGUSTUS' APPROACH to leadership offers timeless lessons that can be directly applied to modern political, corporate, and leadership environments. His ability to consolidate power, maintain stability, and secure long-term loyalty while managing a vast and diverse empire is a masterclass in strategic leadership. Augustus not only used military and political power effectively but also understood the importance of public perception, communication, and balancing competing interests. These lessons can be adapted to today's power structures, offering valuable insights for leaders in any field.

One of Augustus' most important strategies was the careful cultivation of his public image. By portraying himself as a servant of the Roman people rather than a dictator, he was able to maintain widespread support even while holding near-absolute power. Modern leaders, whether in politics or business, can draw from this by recognizing the importance of transparency and perception management. Leaders who position themselves as working for the benefit of their people or organization—and who prioritize the collective good over personal gain—are more likely to garner trust and loyalty. Like Augustus, today's leaders can benefit from framing their authority as a stabilizing force that prioritizes the needs of others.

Augustus' understanding of succession planning also provides valuable lessons for modern organizations. Augustus ensured the continuity of his leadership by carefully grooming and managing potential successors, balancing loyalty and competence. In today's corporate or political settings, leaders who invest in the development of future leaders and ensure a smooth transition of power are more likely to create lasting organizations. Succession planning should be an integral part of long-term strategic thinking, ensuring that key positions are filled with capable individuals who can continue to advance the organization's goals.

Augustus' use of delegation is another key takeaway for modern leadership. He understood the importance of surrounding himself with trusted advisors and capable generals, delegating significant responsibilities while maintaining ultimate control. This is directly applicable to corporate leadership, where effective delegation allows leaders to focus on high-level strategy while empowering others to manage day-to-day operations. By delegating wisely, leaders can avoid burnout, ensure more efficient decision-making, and foster a sense of ownership among their teams—just as Augustus did with figures like Agrippa and Tiberius.

Furthermore, Augustus' ability to balance competing interests is a vital lesson for today's leaders. He managed the delicate relationship between the military, the Senate, and the Roman people by offering each group what it valued most—whether it was stability, financial incentives, or the preservation of Republican traditions. In modern leadership, this translates to understanding the different needs and motivations of various stakeholders. A successful leader must balance the interests of employees, shareholders, customers, and other stakeholders, ensuring that each group feels valued and heard. By aligning the goals of these groups with the organization's overall mission, a leader can maintain cohesion and prevent conflict, much like Augustus balanced the competing powers within Rome.

Finally, Augustus' use of soft power and propaganda to legitimize his rule provides lessons for leaders navigating public relations and media today. Augustus effectively used monuments, literature, and public speeches to craft a narrative that reinforced his authority and framed his rule as divinely ordained. In today's world, leaders must also be mindful of how they shape public perception through media, branding, and communication. Crafting a coherent and positive narrative about one's leadership and vision can significantly influence how they are perceived both internally and externally. By controlling the narrative, as Augustus did, modern leaders can secure their position and maintain public confidence in their leadership.

The practical lessons from Augustus are clear: strategic leadership, effective delegation, succession planning, and managing public perception are as relevant today as they were in ancient Rome. By applying these principles to modern political, corporate, or organizational contexts, leaders can navigate complex environments, foster loyalty, and create lasting legacies. Just as Augustus transformed Rome into a stable empire, today's leaders can use these timeless strategies to build resilient, adaptable, and successful organizations in an ever-changing world.

Universal Principles: The Importance of Perception, Strategic Alliances, and Legal Control in Leadership

AUGUSTUS' REIGN WAS built on several universal principles that remain relevant in today's political, corporate, and leadership environments. Key themes like the importance of managing public perception, building strategic alliances, and maintaining legal control were central to Augustus' success and continue to underpin effective leadership in the modern world. By analyzing how these principles were applied by Augustus and providing contemporary examples, we can see their timeless value.

The importance of perception in leadership cannot be overstated. Augustus understood that how he was seen by the Roman people and elites was as crucial as the actual power he held. By presenting himself as the *Princeps*—a first among equals—rather than an outright ruler or monarch, he managed to wield nearly absolute power while maintaining the appearance of Republican governance. Modern leaders, especially in politics, use similar strategies. For example, successful political figures often present themselves as "public servants" rather than authoritarian figures, even when they hold significant power. Leaders like Franklin D. Roosevelt managed perception effectively by communicating directly with the public through fireside chats, creating the image of a leader deeply connected to the people, while exercising strong executive power behind the scenes.

In the corporate world, perception management is equally crucial. Leaders who shape a positive image for themselves and their companies often maintain a competitive edge. Apple, under Steve Jobs, masterfully curated its image, portraying itself as an innovative and customer-centered company, even as it maintained tight control over its internal processes. The perception of Apple as a cutting-edge and customer-focused brand helped solidify its dominant position in the tech industry. Just as Augustus carefully crafted his image as a leader restoring Roman values and stability, modern leaders must manage how they are perceived to build trust and authority.

Strategic alliances were another cornerstone of Augustus' leadership. He forged key relationships with individuals like Agrippa, his most trusted general, and later with Tiberius, his stepson and eventual successor. These alliances helped him maintain control and stability while ensuring loyalty among the most powerful figures in Roman politics. Today, leaders in business and politics often rely on strategic partnerships to strengthen their position. In politics, alliances between parties, nations, or key figures can make or break a leader's ability to govern. An example of this is the political coalition-building process in parliamentary systems, where leaders must form alliances with other parties to maintain a majority, much like Augustus forged alliances to secure his reign.

In the corporate world, strategic partnerships between companies are common and often essential for success. A notable example is the partnership between Starbucks and various tech companies to integrate their mobile payment systems, allowing Starbucks to stay ahead in a competitive market. These alliances expand influence and resources, ensuring that leaders and organizations can achieve their goals more effectively, just as Augustus' alliances helped him consolidate power and extend his influence across the Roman Empire.

Maintaining legal control was another key theme in Augustus' reign. By using the existing legal framework to his advantage, Augustus presented his consolidation of power as a restoration of the Republic, even while he gradually amassed unprecedented authority. He ensured that the Senate passed laws that gave him supreme control over key provinces and the military, all under the guise of Republicanism.

Today, legal control remains a powerful tool in both politics and business. Political leaders often navigate legal systems to maintain their authority, using laws to legitimize their policies or secure their position. For example, modern governments frequently employ executive orders or emergency powers to pass critical measures quickly, while still operating within the legal framework of their nation.

In the corporate world, maintaining legal control often comes through adherence to regulatory frameworks and corporate governance structures. CEOs and boards of directors must navigate complex legal environments to protect their companies while ensuring compliance. A modern example can be seen in corporate governance strategies employed by multinational companies like Microsoft, which carefully manages its legal obligations across various markets to ensure operational continuity and avoid regulatory penalties. Like Augustus, modern leaders in business must understand and control the legal frameworks in which they operate to secure long-term success.

The universal principles that guided Augustus' leadership—perception management, strategic alliances, and legal control—are just as relevant today as they were in ancient Rome. Whether in politics, business, or other leadership roles, these themes provide a framework for achieving stability, power, and longevity. By mastering these principles, modern leaders can navigate the complexities of today's world with the same strategic foresight that allowed Augustus to build an enduring empire.

Key Takeaway: Augustus' Political Genius Transcends Time, Offering Practical Lessons for Anyone Seeking to Master Leadership and Power

AUGUSTUS' POLITICAL strategies continue to offer valuable lessons for modern leaders in various fields. His ability to blend military power with civilian governance, manage public perception, build strategic alliances, and maintain legal control laid the foundation for a stable and prosperous empire. These skills, refined over decades of rule, demonstrate his unmatched political genius, which transcends time and remains applicable to contemporary leadership.

Leaders today can learn from Augustus' mastery of perception management. By crafting an image of a benevolent leader and servant of the state, Augustus ensured loyalty and minimized opposition. Modern leaders, whether in politics, business, or social movements, must similarly recognize the power of public perception and actively shape it to inspire trust and maintain authority.

Augustus also understood the importance of alliances, not just as temporary political maneuvers but as long-term strategies for stability. His careful selection of loyal generals, politicians, and family members to key roles ensured the continuity of his rule and the future of the empire. In today's complex power structures, strategic partnerships and collaborations are just as critical to achieving lasting success.

Finally, Augustus' use of legal frameworks to legitimize his power illustrates the importance of working within established systems to maintain control. Whether it's navigating corporate governance or political institutions, leaders who can skillfully manage legal and institutional controls are better positioned to create enduring legacies.

In short, Augustus' political genius provides timeless insights into leadership and power. His strategies for managing perception, building alliances, and maintaining legal control are as relevant today as they were in ancient Rome. For anyone seeking to master leadership in any arena, Augustus offers a blueprint for balancing power and stability, ensuring both immediate success and lasting influence.

Conclusion: The Timelessness of Augustus' Political Genius

Summarize Augustus' Political Legacy: Reflecting on Augustus' Blend of Ruthlessness and Subtlety in Shaping Rome's Future

Augustus' political legacy is a testament to his unparalleled ability to blend ruthlessness and subtlety in order to secure and maintain power over the Roman world for decades. Rising to power in the wake of civil war and political chaos, Augustus executed a masterful transformation of Rome from a fractured Republic into a stable empire. His leadership was marked by a shrewd understanding of when to deploy force and when to use diplomacy, allowing him to navigate the political landscape with a deft touch that few rulers in history have matched. His reign set the stage for an era of relative peace and prosperity known as the Pax Romana, which lasted for over 200 years.

Augustus was ruthlessly efficient when it came to removing threats to his power. He eliminated rivals such as Mark Antony, consolidated military control by positioning himself as the commander of Rome's most important legions, and even used legal measures like proscriptions to weaken opposition. However, unlike other leaders who relied solely on brute force, Augustus knew that lasting power required more than defeating enemies—it required managing relationships, cultivating alliances, and maintaining a positive public image. He was adept at using propaganda, carefully managing his public persona as the *Princeps*—Rome's first citizen—rather than a dictator or monarch. This approach allowed him to rule with the appearance of humility while holding absolute authority.

One of Augustus' greatest strengths was his ability to adapt his leadership style to different audiences. To the Senate, he appeared as a restorer of the Republic, offering them a role in governance while quietly centralizing power in his own hands. To the Roman people, he presented himself as a protector and provider, funding public works, games, and grain distributions that enhanced their quality of life and reinforced their loyalty. He strategically balanced the needs of the military, political elites, and common citizens, ensuring that each group felt invested in the stability he brought to Rome. His ability to manipulate the levers of power without alienating key factions is a hallmark of his political genius.

Augustus' subtlety in consolidating power was most evident in how he worked within Rome's traditional institutions to create a new political order without openly dismantling the old one. He retained the Senate as a governing body, but its influence was largely symbolic, as Augustus controlled key provinces and the military. He introduced legal reforms that allowed him to hold offices like consul and tribune while amassing significant personal power. By carefully presenting his actions as restorations of Roman traditions rather than radical changes, Augustus avoided the backlash that often accompanies revolutionary leaders. His reign was not marked by sweeping declarations of autocracy, but by a gradual, calculated accumulation of power that seemed almost natural to his contemporaries.

Succession was another area where Augustus' political acumen shone. Unlike many rulers who failed to plan for life after their death, Augustus carefully groomed and positioned his successors to ensure a smooth transition of power. Though his initial choices—his grandsons Gaius and Lucius—died young, Augustus adapted his plans and selected Tiberius as his heir, ensuring that Rome did not face the chaos of a power vacuum after his death. His use of adoptions and familial alliances helped establish the Julio-Claudian dynasty, which would rule Rome for the next several generations. This careful planning reflected his long-term vision, proving that Augustus was not just focused on his own reign, but on securing the future of the empire.

Augustus' contributions to governance and legal reform are also a significant part of his legacy. He reformed the Roman tax system, created a standing army and navy, and established a system of roads and infrastructure that connected the vast empire. These reforms were critical in transforming Rome from a collection of territories governed by a loose Republic into a cohesive and well-administered empire. By institutionalizing these changes, Augustus laid the groundwork for the Roman Empire's durability and expansion. His legal and administrative innovations would be felt for centuries, providing a model of governance that future emperors would follow.

Perhaps Augustus' most lasting legacy is the stability and peace he brought to Rome after decades of turmoil. The Pax Romana, which began under his reign, allowed Rome to flourish economically, culturally, and militarily. The empire expanded its borders, trade routes stretched across continents, and Roman culture became deeply embedded in the regions under its control. This period of stability allowed Rome to become the superpower of the ancient world, and it was Augustus' careful balancing of military strength, political alliances, and legal reforms that made this possible.

In the end, Augustus' legacy is defined by his ability to create a new political system that ensured the continuity of the Roman Empire long after his death. His skillful combination of ruthlessness and subtlety, force and diplomacy, reform and tradition, allowed him to maintain power for over 40 years. He created a model of leadership that influenced not only the emperors who followed him but also political leaders throughout history. Augustus transformed Rome from a faltering Republic into a stable empire, and his vision, reforms, and strategies set the foundation for centuries of Roman dominance.

Augustus' political genius transcends his time, offering timeless lessons for leaders seeking to balance power, legitimacy, and longevity. His reign illustrates the importance of adapting to changing circumstances, balancing multiple factions, and securing a lasting legacy through careful planning and strategic governance. In shaping the future of Rome, Augustus created an empire whose influence would be felt for centuries, and his political legacy remains one of the most enduring in history.

Final Thoughts: The Enduring Importance of Augustus as a Model for Leadership and Strategic Power in Any Era

AUGUSTUS STANDS AS one of the greatest exemplars of leadership in history, a figure whose political acumen, strategic foresight, and ability to balance power with subtlety continue to resonate across time. His leadership was marked not only by his ability to consolidate and maintain control over a fractured empire but also by his capacity to transform Rome into a stable and prosperous state that would endure for centuries. Augustus understood that true leadership goes beyond immediate victories—it is about creating systems, institutions, and legacies that survive long after a leader's time has passed.

The most remarkable aspect of Augustus' rule was his ability to wield immense power while maintaining the appearance of restoring traditional Republican values. By positioning himself as a servant of the Roman state rather than an autocrat, Augustus avoided the pitfalls of previous leaders like Julius Caesar, who had failed to navigate the delicate balance between power and public perception. Augustus' ability to mask his control under the guise of restoring order and traditional governance is a powerful lesson for modern leaders: managing perception is as important as managing policy. Leaders today, whether in business or politics, must carefully navigate public image, presenting their authority in ways that foster trust and loyalty, even as they consolidate their influence behind the scenes.

Another key takeaway from Augustus' leadership is his masterful use of strategic alliances. Augustus carefully cultivated relationships with key figures—military leaders, politicians, and family members—ensuring their loyalty while positioning them in roles that supported his long-term objectives. This ability to form and maintain alliances, even with potential rivals, is a crucial skill for modern leaders. In today's interconnected and competitive world, successful leaders know that collaboration and coalition-building are essential for achieving and maintaining power. Augustus understood this principle well, surrounding himself with capable allies like Agrippa and Tiberius, and ensuring that the empire would remain stable even after his death.

Augustus also demonstrated the importance of long-term planning, particularly in the realm of succession. Many leaders throughout history have struggled with ensuring a stable transfer of power, but Augustus meticulously prepared for the future of Rome. By grooming successors, arranging key marriages, and controlling the military, Augustus ensured that his legacy would endure. Modern leaders, whether in corporations or governments, must recognize the critical importance of succession planning. A well-managed transition of power is vital for the continued success of any organization, and Augustus provides a blueprint for how to manage this process with foresight and care.

Perhaps Augustus' greatest contribution to leadership is his ability to adapt. Throughout his reign, Augustus continuously adjusted his strategies to meet changing circumstances. Whether it was shifting his plans for succession after the deaths of Gaius and Lucius Caesar or modifying his governance style to keep the Senate and Roman elite on his side, Augustus demonstrated the flexibility that is essential for any long-term leader. Today, adaptability is more critical than ever. Leaders face constantly shifting landscapes—whether economic, political, or social—and the ability to pivot while maintaining a clear vision is a hallmark of effective leadership. Augustus teaches us that being rigid in one's approach can be a downfall, but adapting to challenges while staying true to overarching goals is the key to long-term success.

Augustus' legacy is not just one of political or military triumphs; it is a testament to the art of strategic leadership. His ability to maintain power without alienating the Roman populace, his deft use of alliances, his careful planning for the future, and his adaptability to changing circumstances are all lessons that resonate today. Whether leading a nation, a company, or an organization, Augustus' model of leadership emphasizes the importance of vision, strategy, and the balance between strength and subtlety.

In reflecting on Augustus' leadership, we see the enduring relevance of his principles in any era. His reign, marked by the creation of the Roman Empire's most prosperous and peaceful period, demonstrates that leadership is not just about holding power—it is about using that power wisely, creating lasting structures, and guiding others toward a stable and prosperous future. Augustus' political genius offers timeless lessons for any leader who seeks not just to rise to power, but to sustain it, foster loyalty, and leave a legacy that shapes the future for generations to come. His blend of ruthlessness and subtlety, combined with his long-term vision, sets the standard for leadership that transcends the ages.

Appendix

The following appendix provides additional information, resources, and clarifications related to Augustus' reign, leadership principles, and their relevance to modern leadership. It serves as a supplemental guide to deepen the understanding of Augustus' political strategies, offering further insights into the historical context of his decisions and how they continue to apply in various sectors today.

1. Timeline of Key Events in Augustus' Reign

- **44 BCE**: Assassination of Julius Caesar. Octavian, later Augustus, emerges as his heir.

- **43 BCE**: Formation of the Second Triumvirate between Octavian, Mark Antony, and Lepidus.

- **31 BCE**: Battle of Actium. Octavian defeats Mark Antony and Cleopatra, consolidating his control over Rome.

- **27 BCE**: The *First Settlement*. Octavian is granted the title Augustus by the Senate, marking the beginning of the Roman Empire.

- **23 BCE**: The *Second Settlement*. Augustus receives tribunician power and proconsular imperium, securing his authority.

- **2 BCE**: Augustus is named *Pater Patriae* (Father of the Fatherland).

- **14 CE**: Augustus dies, and Tiberius succeeds him as emperor.

2. Key Titles and Powers of Augustus

- **Princeps**: Meaning "first citizen," this title allowed Augustus to position himself as a leader without the connotations of monarchy or dictatorship.

- **Imperator**: A title given to victorious military commanders, reinforcing his role as the supreme leader of the Roman legions.

- **Tribunicia Potestas**: Tribunician power granted him the ability to veto laws and introduce legislation, consolidating civil control.

- **Proconsular Imperium**: Allowed Augustus to govern the most militarily significant provinces, securing control over the empire's military forces.

- **Pontifex Maximus**: As the chief priest, Augustus positioned himself as the religious leader of Rome, merging religious and political authority.

3. The Pax Romana: Augustus' Lasting Legacy

AUGUSTUS' REIGN USHERED in the Pax Romana, a period of relative peace and stability across the Roman Empire that lasted for over two centuries. The following sections highlight the key features of this era:

- **Economic Growth**: With secure borders and reduced internal conflict, trade and commerce flourished under Augustus' rule. Infrastructure such as roads, ports, and aqueducts were expanded, integrating the empire's territories more efficiently.

- **Cultural Flourishing**: Literature, art, and architecture thrived during this period. Augustus patronized poets like Virgil and Horace, contributing to the cultural renaissance that celebrated Roman values and Augustus' leadership.

- **Military Stability**: Augustus reduced the size of the Roman army but made it more professional, establishing a standing force and creating the *aerarium militare*, a treasury for paying veterans.

---

4. The Use of Propaganda in Augustus' Reign

AUGUSTUS WAS A MASTER of propaganda, using various media to shape his public image and solidify his power. Some of the key examples include:

- **Statues and Monuments**: Public works such as the Ara Pacis (Altar of Peace) and statues of Augustus as both a military leader and a benevolent ruler helped cultivate the image of Augustus as the savior and protector of Rome.

- **Coins**: Augustus frequently used coins to propagate his image, often depicting himself alongside Roman gods or

Page

military symbols to emphasize his divine favor and military prowess.

- **Literature**: Virgil's *Aeneid* was commissioned by Augustus to create a mythic connection between himself and Rome's legendary founder, Aeneas. This association underscored Augustus' role as the restorer of Roman greatness.

5. Leadership Principles from Augustus' Reign and Their Modern Applications

- **Perception Management**: Augustus carefully managed public perception, presenting himself as a humble leader restoring Republican values while holding ultimate authority. In modern contexts, effective leaders recognize the importance of how they are perceived by employees, stakeholders, and the public.

- **Strategic Alliances**: Augustus formed alliances with key figures such as Agrippa and Tiberius, ensuring loyalty and stability. Today, strategic partnerships within industries, politics, or organizations are essential for building support and achieving long-term goals.

- **Succession Planning**: By grooming his successors and controlling the future of Rome, Augustus ensured stability after his death. Modern leaders must also plan for future transitions to maintain organizational continuity and success.

6. Key Figures in Augustus' Political Landscape

- **Marcus Agrippa**: Augustus' close friend, trusted general, and advisor. Agrippa's military success at Actium and his role in urban development in Rome were crucial to Augustus' reign.

- **Livia Drusilla**: Augustus' wife and political confidante, who played a significant role in shaping the imperial family and influencing succession plans.

- **Tiberius**: Augustus' stepson and eventual successor, who was adopted to secure the continuity of the Julio-Claudian dynasty.

- **Germanicus**: A popular general and relative of Augustus, Germanicus was positioned as a potential successor and later served as a model of Roman military leadership.

7. Modern Leadership Comparisons

- **Political Leadership**: Augustus' ability to maintain a balance between autocracy and Republican ideals can be compared to modern democratic leaders who balance power and representation. Leaders like Franklin D. Roosevelt managed public perception and wielded executive power effectively during crises, much like Augustus did during the transformation of Rome.

- **Corporate Leadership**: Augustus' strategic planning, delegation, and focus on long-term stability resonate with corporate leaders like Steve Jobs, who focused on innovation, succession, and the careful cultivation of a company's public image.

● **Military Leadership**: Augustus' control over the military while ensuring that no individual general gained too much power has parallels in modern military structures, where commanders are rotated to prevent the consolidation of independent power bases.

---

8. Further Reading and Resources

● **Books**:

○ *Augustus: The Life of Rome's First Emperor* by Anthony Everitt.

○ *The Twelve Caesars* by Suetonius (focuses on the lives of Augustus and subsequent emperors).

○ *Res Gestae Divi Augusti*: Augustus' own account of his achievements, offering insight into how he wished to be remembered.

● **Online Resources**:

○ The Cambridge Ancient History Volume X: The Augustan Empire 43 BC–AD 69.

○ Digital copies of Roman coins featuring Augustus, hosted by various museum collections, showcasing his use of visual propaganda.